Buddhist Symbolism in *Tibetan Thangkas*

Buddhist Symbolism in Tibetan Thangkas

The Story of Siddhartha and other Buddhas
Interpreted in Modern Nepalese Painting

– Ben Meulenbeld

Binkey Kok Publications – Havelte/Holland

Published by Binkey Kok Publications BV
Hofstede De Weide Hoek – Havelte/Holland

Fax: 31-521591925
E-mail: binkey@inn.nl
English translation copyright © 2001 Binkey Kok Publications

ISBN 90-74597-44-0

Translated by Wanda Boeke
Editing: Valerie Cooper
Photography: Eelco Boeijinga, Ben Meulenbeld
Layout and cover design: Jaap Koning
Printed and bound in the Netherlands

Distributed in the U.S.A. by Samuel Weiser Inc.
P. O. Box 612, York Beach, Maine 03910-0162

Contents

Acknowledgments – viii
Introduction – ix

**I Purpose & Creation
of the Thangka – 1**
Origin – 1
Function – 1
Theme and Composition – 1
Art or Craft? – 2
The Making of a Thangka – 2

II Religious Background – 7
Northern India 2,600 Years Ago – 7
Siddhartha Gautama – 7
From Siddhartha to
    Shakyamuni: The Life of the Buddha – 7

III Theravada Buddhism – 18
Shakyamuni Buddha
    with Shariputra and Maudgalyayana – 18

IV Mahayana Buddhism – 21
The Buddha with Dhyani Buddhas – 24
Series of Buddhas – 24
Medicine Buddhas – 28
Bhaisajyaguru – 30
A Medicinal Thangka – 30
The Medicine Buddha – 30
The Eighteen Arhats – 35
Avalokiteshvara & other Bodhisattvas – 37
Shadakshari Lokeshvara – 38
Sahasrabhuja Lokeshvara – 38
Manjushri – 41
The White Tara – 43
The Green Tara – 46

V Vajrayana Buddhism – 47
Basic Principles of Vajrayana Buddhism – 47
The Demise of Buddhism in India – 48
Padmasambhava – 48
Guru Rinpoche – 49
The Mystical Padmasambhava – 49
The Eight Guises of Padmasambhava – 52
Dakinis and Yoginis – 54
Sarvabuddha Yogini – 54
Mahasiddha Tilopa – 54

Mahasiddha Naropa – 57
Milarepa – 59
The Wheel of Life – 64
Gathering of Saints – 66
Tsongkhapa – 72
Yidams and Dharmapalas – 72
Kalachakra – 73
Chakrasamvara – 73
Herukas – 73
Mandalas – 76
The Mandala of Yama – 78
The Kalachakra Mandala – 80
The All-powerful Ten Mandala – 82

VI Paubhas – 85
Vasudhara – 85

Glossary – 89
Bibliography – 95
Index – 96

Illustrations

Plates

1. The Life of the Buddha – 9
2. The Life of the Buddha – 11
3. The Life of the Buddha – 13
4. The Life of the Buddha – 15
5. The Shakyamuni Buddha with Shariputra and Maudgalyayana – 19
6. The Buddha with Dhyani Buddhas – 23
7. Series of Buddhas – 25
8. Series of Buddhas – 27
9. Series of Buddhas – 28
10. Bhaisajyaguru, the Medicine Buddha – 31
11. Medicinal Thangka – 32
12. Medicine Buddha – 33
13. The Eighteen Arhats – 36
14. The Bodhisattva Shadakshari Lokeshvara – 39
15. The Bodhisattva Sahasrabhuja Lokeshvara – 40
16. The Bodhisattva Manjushri – 42
17. The White Tara – 44
18. The Green Tara – 45
19. Guru Rinpoche – 50
20. The Mystical Padmasambhava – 51
21. The Eight Guises of Padmasambhava – 53
22. Sarvabuddha Yogini – 55
23. The Mahasiddha Tilopa – 56
24. The Mahasiddha Naropa – 58
25. Milarepa – 60
26. Milarepa – 62
27. The Wheel of Life – 65
28. The Wheel of Life – 67
29. Gathering of Saints – 68
30. Tsongkhapa – 70
31. Kalachakra – 74
32. Chakrasamvara – 75
33. Herukas – 77
34. The Mandala of Yama – 79
35. The Kalachakra Mandala – 81
36. The All-powerful Ten Mandala – 83
37. Vasudhara – 87

Figures

1. Stretched and prepared canvas – 3
2. A sketch – 3
3. Sketches and templates – 3
4. Adding color to the drawing – 3
5. A thangka in a brocade frame – 5
6. 35 Confessional Buddhas – 26
7. Eight Medicine Buddhas – 26
8. Monastery entrance – 34
9. OM MANI PADME HUM – 38
10. Vajra and ghanta – 72

Acknowledgments

A word of thanks to: *Dick Plukker* for many useful and remedial recommendations; Tibetologist *Sjoerd de Vries* for his elucidating comments; *Margriet Hamacher* and *Tara Meulenbeld* for their enormous patience; and *Binkey Kok* for his inexhaustible perseverance.

Introduction

The great Italian authority on Tibet, Giuseppe Tucci first published his Tibetan Painted Scrolls, the standard three-volume text on thangkas, in 1949. In his preface he asserts that the Tibetan art of painting should expect far less appreciation than the Indian or Persian.

During the fifty years that have passed since Tucci wrote his book, this evaluation has changed a good deal. Appreciation for Tibetan art and painting has been significantly on the rise. Thangkas have become more and more popular among art lovers and collectors, due to an increased interest in Tibet and Tibetan Buddhism. Tragically, this interest gained momentum after the Chinese annexation of Tibet in 1959, and the subsequent exodus and diaspora of Tibetans to Nepal, India, and other countries. The catastrophic Chinese Cultural Revolution sounded the death knell for native Tibetan culture. Monasteries and the art housed within them were destroyed. Much of what escaped the mad demolition was sold to the Western art market.

The prices of the old and beautiful thangkas that were smuggled out of Tibet spiraled upward in the high-price bidding for antique art. These paintings go for fabulous sums at auctions and galleries, and grace numerous public and private collections in the West and in Japan.

The demand for older, 12th- to 15th-century thangkas has led to extremely clever forgeries, often on old canvases. The recent demand for paintings from the 18th and 19th centuries created a new series of imitations, all but indistinguishable from authentic works.

Around 1965, a second "Awakening of the East" began with the rise of international tourism in Southern Asia. The popularity of a destination such as Nepal began at this time. Many Nepalese, and even Tibetan refugees in Nepal, began to devote themselves to doing business in religious objects. One favorite tourist item turned out to be the easily transported, easily rolled up, lightweight painting of exotic gods and tableaux, the thangka. Painting thangkas became a flourishing industry. Tourists would buy a hurriedly painted thangka in Kathmandu to take with them as a souvenir. Back at home, many began to immerse themselves in the imagery, comparing their thangkas with others. Often they discovered the many differences in the quality and value of the thangka paintings.

Now, there is a large group of collectors who won't, or can't, spend five to ten thousand dollars or more on an antique or a cleverly forged thangka, but who also don't want to have a lifeless painting that only costs twenty. The market is aware of this, and in the Kathmandu Valley, higher quality thangkas are being made that contain more varied themes than the hasty, lifeless ones that can be purchased in street bazaars.

This introductory book displays and explains a number of Buddhist scenes, tableaux, and themes that are frequently seen and sought-after in Tibetan thangkas. It provides the technical, religious, and iconographic backgrounds of the paintings. I have tried to apply some kind of structure to the apparent chaos of the divine world that they portray. I have also simplified several difficult themes and concepts, including Tantrism and Vajrayana Buddhism, in order to convey their most essential elements.

The material in this book is based on a large private collection of thangkas painted in the Kathmandu Valley in Nepal. Some of the painters are Tibetan. Since the exodus, many Tibetans live in Nepal. Their newly built monasteries, such as the now-famous Bodnath, have been decorated according to their ancient traditions. The new monasteries have also continued the tradition of monks painting thangkas. Most thangka painters, however, are Tamang and Newari. Both of these Nepalese peoples live primarily in and around the Kathmandu Valley. The Valley measures only 13 by 20 miles (20 by 30 kilometers), and although there are dozens of villages and towns there, the metropolis of Kathmandu is the heart of the valley and its economic activity.

The Tamang are Buddhists who have an old artistic tradition. Their priests are known for painting thangkas. However, in today's urban economy, many thangkas are done primarily by Tamang who are not priests.

The Newari, likewise, constitute a Buddhist population in a mostly Hindu area. They have a strong, long-standing affinity with the Tibetans. Newari always did business with Tibet and significantly contributed to the development of Tibetan art. Aniko, who created numerous works of art during the 13th century in Tibet, is legendary. Newari artists used to paint (and still do) for Tibetan monasteries and Tibetan clients in the Katmandu Valley. Moreover, in more recent centuries, Newari art has experienced influences from Tibet and China that have also contributed to stylistic developments in Tibet over the past 300 years.

Tibetan refugees spread out over large portions of Southern Asia. Many live and work in the heat of Southern India. Others had the luck—relatively speaking—of ending up on the cool flanks of the Northern Indian Himalayas, in places such as Dharamsala, Mussoorie, or Manali. Beautiful thangkas are painted here, and the work is often done in a manner that is in keeping with the old and revered Tibetan painting styles.

Tourists have certainly not been the only target group for modern-day Nepalese thangkas. Besides being used in monasteries, thangkas are also hung above the altars of Buddhist homes, where the paintings have a function in the family's daily religious practice. For special celebrations such as religious festivals, specific thangkas are unrolled, to be especially venerated at that time.

This collection of thangkas contains diverse variations of some subjects, few of others, and still other themes have been entirely omitted. Sometimes small, subsidiary figures and scenes appear in the thangkas. Although they may seem insignificant, they are discussed at length due to their iconographic importance.

In the descriptions of the paintings in this book, when "left" or "right" is stated, it is meant from the point of view of the person looking at the picture. A reversal of this is when, for instance, the text reads "to the right of the Buddha," which indicates something or someone to his right (from his point of view), which is the viewer's left.

Since readability is of primary importance in this book, the diacritical marks in Sanskrit words have been left out, and names such as Shakyamuni and Avalokiteshvara are printed without the accent on the "S." The Tibetan Buddhist culture largely derives from India, so the use of Sanskrit names and words is acceptable and customary. Therefore, Chenrezi is referred to as Avalokiteshvara (the former name is Tibetan), and Man-la, the medicine buddha, is called Bhaisajyaguru. "Vajra," is used here instead of "dorje," for the magical-religious attribute of the thunder-dagger.

Sometimes, however, the Tibetan concepts are more familiar. In this case, I have used, for instance, "yidam" instead of the Sanskrit "ishtadevata" when referring to a personal guardian deity. Tibetan names and words have been rendered phonetically, giving us "Gelugpa" and "Kadampa," instead of "dGe Lugs Pa" and "bKa' Gdams Pa." However, even on a phonetic level there are different possible transcriptions, such as Songtsen Gampo, Srong Tsen Ganpo, or Srongtsen Ganbo. While neither unanimity nor uniformity is feasible, consistency has been the goal.

Within the limited scope of a short book such as this one, the opinions and explications set forth are, of necessity, a compilation of many views. Different schools, sects, and authorities on this material contributed to a variety of interpretations over the course of centuries. In this brief introduction to the art of Tibetan Buddhism, it will become clear that, in Eastern religious philosophy, there are literally many ways to view the truth!

I / Purpose & Creation of the Thangka

The roots of Tibetan Buddhism lie in India. Tibetan art is mainly religious, and its form and meaning also initially originated in India. Nepal functioned both as a filter and as a conveyor of new artistic ideas. Toward the end of the 17th century, China added aesthetic elements to the art and culture of Tibet.

The first significant contact Tibet had with Buddhism was in the seventh century, when the powerful King Songtsen Gampo (617-649) married Buddhist princesses from Nepal and T'ang China. In the beginning, Buddhism was practiced by the king and a few of the nobility. King Trisong Detsen (second half of the eighth century) did much to breathe new life into the slumbering Buddhism, including inviting the tantric master Padmasambhava to his inner court.

In the ninth century, Buddhism experienced a temporary setback under the apostate Langdarma, but after his death, its development gathered new momentum.

Origin

With the tenth century began what is called "The Second Coming of Buddhism" from Western Tibet into the whole of Tibet. Indian holy men brought theological renewal and artistic ideas to Tibet. At the same time, Tibetan scholars were going to study in Buddhist Kashmir and at the great Buddhist monastic universities in Northeast India. They returned by way of Ladakh and Nepal with religious literature and artists. In their view, artists were of importance because the bulk of the people could gain little from complicated theological discourses. Seeing the new belief was more important, and much more effective.

In India and Nepal at that time, paintings known as patas and paubhas, showing symbols and depictions of deities and saints, were used, among other things, to visualize difficult theory. Storytellers would roll these paintings out and provide an explanation of the imagery. Patas still appear sporadically in India in a slightly different form, while paubhas are now made and used by the Buddhist Newari minority in the Kathmandu Valley (see Plate 37 on page 87). This notion of "show and tell" lies at the basis of the thangka, which derived from the pata and the paubha.

Function

A thangka is a scroll painting. The Tibetan word thangka means "something that can be rolled up." On annual market days and at celebrations, in villages and pilgrimage sites, traveling monks and lamas unrolled thangkas and told stories about saints and deities as they pointed out elements in the painted tableaux. For protection and liturgical reasons, pilgrims and travelers would take a rolled-up thangka along on their perilous journeys. Both uses are still in practice, but to a lesser degree than several generations ago.

The most important function of a thangka is as a religious aid in ritual actions, or as a guideline and a help in meditation. By seeing the figures depicted, concentrating on them, and identifying with the central deity or personage, the believer strives for "liberation through beholding." This identification is simplified for the concentrated believer if he or she can become immersed in and completely identify with all the details of the main and secondary figures. Thangkas thus provide, in visual form, precise iconographic information that the meditator can utilize.

But thangkas are more than religious visual aids. They are also commissioned when problems such as illness, death, or abstract obstacles—in personal or social matters—-arise in a family. The painting is then hung up with the expectation that a protective or positive force will radiate from it, and the thangka thereby gains the function of a "lucky charm" or amulet. This is why some thangkas display nothing but lucky symbols, astrological configurations, or medicinal plants.

Theme and Composition

Clients indicate which scene they want and which deities and personages are essential. Often, their guru, or spiritual mentor, will be the motivating guide in choosing the theme and its corresponding elements. The painter determines the composition. The painter will work out which figures will be prominently portrayed, in what kind of (fantasy) landscape they will be situated, and where architectural elements and details will be included. Most painters are laypersons. They have a reasonably broad knowledge of iconography and base what they do on descriptions in books of rites. For exceptional cases, monks or other religious specialists are consulted.

The composition is usually symmetrical, with the main figure in the middle of an imaginary vertical axis. Less important personages and deities are grouped on both sides and are smaller. Hierarchy is a principle that carries a lot of weight. In thangkas composed of various types of figures, spiritual leaders and gurus will occupy the foremost position. The supreme teacher or primary divinity of a religious system or sect will appear at the very top of the picture. Then, in order of decreasing importance, come yidams, buddhas, bodhisattvas, dakinis, dharmapalas, lokapalas, and lesser deities.

The composition is adapted to the number of figures desired. Modern thangkas are becoming more flexible in the placement of personages and in the details.

The Tibetan pantheon also has a hierarchy of sizes. Depending on someone's importance, that person will be painted larger or smaller. Depending on the school the painter follows, the number of size categories will vary from four to eleven. Painters know the sizes and accompanying characteristic traits of the primary deities and figures. The unknown ones can be found in books and tables. Body parts, such as hands, feet, and hips, have a standard size, and the distances between things, such as from the tip of the nose to the chin, are set as well.

Art or Craft?

Adherents to Tibetan Buddhism are interested only in the religious aspects of the thangka, not in its artistic aspect. The painting functions merely as an aid. The concept of "art" plays no part. This also explains why a thangka can hang in a nomad's smoky tent, above a house altar's clarified butter lamps with their greasy smoke, under a leaking monastery roof so that the canvas becomes water-stained, or can be packed, rolled,

or folded up and taken on a trip. It is a tool. The maker of a thangka is seen as a painter, not as an artist. This same person will also paint masks, furniture, or parts of houses. The maker will usually be a devout layperson of the male gender. The profession is often hereditary. Thangkas are seldom, if ever, signed.

Originally, most of the non-Tibetan collectors went for exotic and artistic qualities first. To an ever greater degree, the need to know background information has become of additional importance. The Western collector seldom keeps thangkas rolled up, but will hang them on the wall, for aesthetic reasons.

The Making of a Thangka

Most thangkas are painted on a canvas. Some are painted on paper or leather. Others are embroidered, appliquéd, woven, and patchwork thangkas, but these forms are not discussed here. Technically, making a painted thangka occurs in four stages:

1) *preparing the foundation*
2) *sketching*
3) *painting*
4) *framing*

Preparing the Foundation

The kind of thangka under discussion here, the canvas you buy, is made of a woven material: cotton, linen, and sometimes silk. A finely woven structure, made of a single piece of fabric, is best, because paint easily chips off of thicker or rougher fabrics when the thangka is rolled up. The painted canvas is rectangular in shape, taller than it is wide, ideally measuring on the average 30 inches tall by 20 inches wide (75 by 50 centimeters). The same 3:2 ratio of height to width can also be found in other formats: 12 by 8 inches (30 by 20 cm); 48 by 32 inches (120 by 80 cm); 120 by 80 inches (300 by 200 cm) for exceptionally large specimens. These proportions generally also apply to the huge thangkas—measuring up to 180 by 130 feet (55 by 40 meters)—that are hung outside the walls of the monasteries during festivals. There are also elongated thangkas that are wider

Figure 1. Stretched and prepared canvas

Figure 2. A sketch

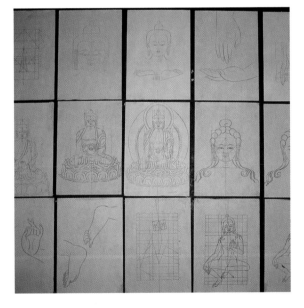

Figure 3. Sketches and templates

Figure 4. Adding color to the drawing

than they are tall (see Plates 4 and 13, pages 15 and 36, respectively), with a size ratio of 2:3.

The edges of the canvas are folded over twice, rather than hemmed, to prevent them from unraveling. Then the canvas is fastened with thread to four laths that are firmly attached with twine to a wooden frame, and strung tightly, so that it looks like an upright trampoline.

The front and the back of the cloth are swabbed with a sizing of animal glue consisting of boiled bones and skins, often of a water buffalo. After this dries, the cloth is painted with a pasty gesso, a mixture of lime or rice flour, and plaster or chalk. After this layer has been applied, it is polished with a smooth stone or shell. This produces a smooth, even layer on rough or uneven cloth that will function well for sketching and painting, and will keep the paint from seeping into the cloth.

Sketching

For orientation, the painter will often first lay down a grid of coordinates in the form of eight lines: two diagonal lines with a horizontal and a vertical axis drawn through their intersection, and four lines drawn parallel to the frame. Sometimes the painter will do this on the back so that the lines show through when the canvas is held up to the light. The next step is a charcoal sketch. When the painter is satisfied with the result, the lines will be accentuated with ink.

There are separate drawings, or templates, available for many of the figures that are to be painted. They can be transferred to the canvas by pricking holes through them along the contours and on the most important lines and components. Powder is blown through these holes, resulting in a dotted outline on the canvas. Another technique for transferring figures uses block prints. The wood or metal blocks are painted black; the figures are colored in at a later stage.

Painting

When the sketch is finished, it is time for the coloring stage. Large color areas are often applied by students or assistants. Instructions are given by brushing or writing numbers or syllables into the area in question. Black, for instance, is indicated with the number two or with the syllable Na, yellow with five, or Sa. When applying the colors, a particular sequence is commonly followed. First, the area furthest away in perspective, the sky, is colored. Then the closer landscape is done, followed by trees, rocks, and water. After this come the deities and other figures. The throne, clothing, and nimbus are painted first. Light colors are applied before dark colors, and then details in gold are added.

Painting is done as economically as possible in order to avoid constantly preparing or mixing paint. If the painter is using a particular color, it will be applied to all the relevant places, sometimes to several thangkas at once. Shadows are worked in toward the end. Finally, the faces are painted—the eyes last of all. As with sculptures, after the eyes have been rendered, "the opening of the eyes" is an important initiation ceremony, celebrated, incidentally, only for special thangkas. Before the 19th century, only mineral pigments and organic coloring agents were used. Even today pigments are still being produced in this way, but faster and cheaper alternatives have come along. At the beginning of the 19th century, the development of synthetic colors got underway in Europe. The motivation was finding an alternative for the expensive color blue produced from lapis lazuli and ultramarine (ground lazurite). Since 1850, synthetic pigments have been making their way to India and beyond, including Nepal and Tibet.

The colors are put in ceramic or porcelain bowls. A little binding agent is added—most often a lime made of boiled animal skins, along with a little bit of water—and it all gets heated up slowly.

Today's thangkas are increasingly made using modern colors. Factory-made paints offer a great variety of colors and tints. The present generation of Tibetans and Newari painters are in no way averse to using them and are experimenting to their hearts' content.

There are five basic colors: red, yellow, green, blue, and white. Another important color that is widely used is black.

Many of the paintings reproduced here exhibit modern color schemes. They have been done with water-based paints. Often, but not always, a layer of vegetable varnish is applied.

Besides polychromatic paintings, there are gold thangkas with gold backgrounds and drawings done in red, with very little or no additional color. In general, peace-loving deities and personages are depicted in gold thangkas. Then there are black thangkas, made with a blue-black ink as a base, and a minimal amount of color; this presentation usually consists of wrathful deities. There are also red thangkas with a lot of gold details, depicting friendly or protective deities.

Paint is applied with brushes of various sizes. They have wooden handles that have been cut to a point on one side. Hairs are tied around the point. The hair can be from a goat, cat, or horse. In Nepal, hairs taken from the ears of water buffaloes are most often used. Painters today also use imported factory-made brushes.

Framing

Once the painting is finished, the canvas is loosened from its stretchers and framed with textile edging. The silk or brocade trim is of an established width, so that the depth of the bottom trim is half the length of the painting, the top one-fourth, and the sides are one-eighth of the length. Still, the framed thangka is not completely rectangular but splays out a little toward the bottom.

At the top, the silk frame is stitched around a wooden lath along its entire width. A smooth dowel that protrudes an inch or so on both sides is similarly mounted at the bottom, and metal caps are usually slipped over the ends. If a thangka is not in use, but not rolled up either, a thin piece of silk may hang in front of the image to protect it from soot and smoky lamps, and to avoid the image being visually touched by uninitiated eyes. Often the curtain will be yellow silk, with red or blue dots, or sometimes it has a flower motif on it. Over this lowered curtain two bands

Figure 5. Thangka in brocade frame

of red silk hang down to the very bottom. At the top between these two strips hangs a lightweight red cord with which the veil can be tied up. At the very top there is a cord by which the thangka can be hung or with which it can be tied together when it is rolled up.

II / Religious Background

Over 3,500 years ago, the Arya, who were Central-Asian cattle nomads, entered the Indian subcontinent. Over the course of centuries they settled down in the north, made inhospitable ground arable, and became farmers. Their religion, Vedism, developed from the veneration of natural phenomena—utilizing burnt offerings and animal sacrifices—into the complex religious system, with its many philosophies and numerous deities, which we know today as Hinduism. Gradually, the sacrifices became so complicated that the people could no longer make them independently, and had to call on the help of Brahmans, religious specialists, who ensured good communication with the deities.

Northern India 2,600 Years Ago

After almost one thousand years, an aversion to the complicated, abstract sacrifices and the hegemony of the Vedic priests developed among the populace. In addition to this came the combination of the caste system, a Brahman idea, with its rigid rules and laws of conduct that limited social interaction, and the emerging belief in the eternally revolving wheel of rebirth. For the average person, escape from the cycle of reincarnation, or samsara, was all but impossible. Anyone leading a life of woe could count on a similarly miserable life during the next sojourn on earth. Hardly an inspiring outlook! What determines the nature of rebirth is a person's karma. During life, every person builds up karma. Karma is the sum of all one's acts and thoughts, of all positive and negative deeds. Reactions to what was for many a dead-end perspective arose sometime between the seventh and the sixth centuries b.c.e., and manifested themselves in protest and reform movements. One of the social responses that offered a chance of escape from being endlessly reborn we know under a term that was coined much later: Buddhism.

Siddhartha Gautama

The person who we call "the Buddha" was born around 560 b.c.e., in Lumbini, as Siddhartha Gautama. His "first name" was Siddhartha, Gautama was his family name. His father, Shuddho-

dana, was the ruler of the Shakyas, a small tribe in southern Nepal. Later, when Siddhartha had become a religious sage—a muni—he received the honorific title of Shakyamuni. He died around 480 b.c.e.

After the death of Shakyamuni Buddha, his closest followers continued his teaching. But, just as with the other systems of thought existing at that time, there was no material expression of the teachings at all, or to put it plainly, there was no iconography. As of the third century before our era, the figurative arts began to develop. However, in Buddhism, by reason of respect, people did not dare to portray the Buddha (compare with Islam on this level). Symbols such as the rendition of his footprints or of a throne, empty but for a turban such as he had worn during his princely life, sufficed.

Shortly after the beginning of our era, an image of the Buddha was created. Portrayals of important moments in the life of Shakyamuni quickly followed. These scenes gradually became grouped together, and around the fifth century, visual arts showed groupings of four or eight major moments or major events.

From Siddhartha to Shakyamuni: The Life of the Buddha

In Tibetan painting, a series of twelve major moments in the Buddha's life developed. The iconographic sequence is standard, but the location of the tableaux in the paintings may vary. Sometimes scenes are added or omitted, as is evident in the thangkas in Plates 1 through 4 on pages 9, 11, 13, and 15. These twelve important moments give us an overview of Siddhartha, the person who became Shakyamuni, and of his Buddhist teachings. The twelve official events are:

1) *Queen Maya's dream*
2) *The birth of Siddhartha*
3) *Raising the young prince*
4) *Life at the court*
5) *The four encounters*
6) *Siddhartha secretly leaves the palace*
7) *Asceticism*
8) *Mara's attack*

9) Enlightenment

10) Proclaiming the teachings

11) Extraordinary events

12) Parinirvana

Queen Maya's Dream

In the upper left corner of the thangkas in Plates 1 through 4 is the sleeping Queen Maya, who dreamed of a white elephant that flew through the air and touched her right side with its trunk. Elephants are well-known for their strength and intelligence, but are also associated with gray rain clouds and so with fertility, because rainwater means that seeds will germinate and vegetables will be able to grow. A white elephant adds to this an element of purity and immaculacy. The royal fortunetellers explained that the dream announced the queen's pregnancy and that the newborn would possess exceptional traits. In former lives, the Buddha had been an elephant several times. This white elephant can be seen as the future Buddha himself who descends from heaven so that he can be born.

It was prophesied that he would become a chakravartin. *Chakravartin* means "wheel turner." A golden wheel, or chakra—a rim with four, eight, or more spokes—is an ancient Indian symbol of universal authority. Anyone who turns this symbolic wheel exercises authority. In a secular sense, a gold wheel is thought to roll out before a great and ideal ruler in order to conquer the world for him without violence. On a sacred level, however, a person can also be a conqueror and turn the wheel of religious teachings.

To the left, below the palace with the dreaming queen, it is evident that right after her pregnancy was made known, Maya was congratulated and offered gifts. In order to fortify her, she was fed by the gods for ten months.

The Birth of Siddhartha

As her due date approached, Maya took a trip to her parental home to have the baby there with her mother, an ancient custom that is still practiced. However, the contractions set in en route, and, in a garden in present-day Lumbini in Southern Nepal, the crown prince was born out of his mother's right side. It is believed that, in all

things, right is more positive than left. When we see how the birth took place and recall that Queen Maya died seven days later, it is not impossible that this was an instance of royal birth by caesarian section. Indian doctors were renowned in antiquity, but they wouldn't have had much understanding of germs and hygiene.

In the scene of the birth, the queen grabs hold of a tree and bends a branch down. This motif is common in older Indian art. If a young woman grasps a tree branch this way, it is said the tree will burst into bloom. Taking this image one level further, it means that she herself is bursting into bloom, which indicates fertility and pregnancy.

The Hindu gods Brahma and Indra were present at the birth. Normally, in Hinduism, everything that has to do with death, birth, excrement, and blood, is unclean. The fact that the two main gods of Hinduism were assisting should not only be interpreted politically, but also indicates that this was a non-defiling birth. In Plates 1 and 2, Brahma can clearly be recognized by his four heads (three are visible, the fourth one is on the other side). In Plate 1, Indra stands ready to wrap the baby in a cloth.

The little child was exceptional. He raised his right index finger, took seven steps (lotuses spring forth beneath his feet), and announced that he had been born for the last time and would attempt to eliminate suffering in the world. Deities heard his words and blessed him from heaven with a cleansing bath (see the vertical golden line in Plate 2) and showers of flowers (Plate 3).

Everywhere that same day miracles manifested themselves. The blind were able to see again, the lame could walk. An illuminating glow surrounded the earth and a pleasant fragrance descended. That day, 84,000 boys were born. Everything that is great and big is always given the number 84,000. And in Southern Asia, the feeling that boys are more important than girls is still amply evident. Afterward, mother and child went to the palace (Plates 1 and 2, lower left).

Raising the Young Prince

The wise Asita paid his respects and saw that he was encountering a great and universal ruler

Plate 1. The Life of the Buddha

because the little boy had 32 unusual, characteristic physical features (lakshanas) and 80 characteristic aesthetic traits. In art, only a few of the 32 are to be clearly visualized: a gold glow around the body; a blue-black shine to the hair; wavy hair growing to the right; his bulging fontanel (ushnisha) covered with hair; a face bright as the full moon; a lock of hair curling onto his forehead; a swastika on his chest; straight shoulders; chakras in the palms of his hands and soles of his feet; arms reaching down to his knees; long slender fingers; soft palms with a silk-like sheen; hidden genitals; good body proportions.

The other characteristic physical features are soft hair, hair and body free of dust, skin tone of freshly opened flowers, purple eyes with a gentle expression, forty perfect, straight, white teeth, a tongue as broad as a lotus, sweet-tasting saliva, a melodious voice, jaws and rib cage like a lion's, calves of a deer, dragon's thighs, well-joined golden bones, flat chest, straight, flat feet. This list is not unequivocal. Sometimes lakshanas and aesthetic traits get mixed up. We could also mention thick, dark eyebrows in a perfect arc; calm well-formed eyes that smile; straight nose placed high on the face; red curved lips; tapering fingers and toes with webs between them; slender waist.

By virtue of the lakshanas, Asita foretold that the boy would become a great holy man. Reflecting on this and the earlier chakravartin prophecy, King Shuddhodana saw little good to be had from a son who was going to devote himself to spiritually and morally lofty things. He wanted Siddhartha to be the successor to his realm and so decided to protect the crown prince from the outside world and to surround him with all manner of luxuries and temptations. The king hoped that a hedonistic and carefree life would prevent the crown prince from broadening his horizons beyond the walls of the palace complex, and that he would never devote himself to philosophical reflections (Plate 3, left, center). But the prince had little interest in glamour, splendor, or entertainment.

King Shuddhodana was disappointed that the prince did not seem to derive any pleasure from all the luxury, preferring to daydream and meditate under a tree. His councilors advised providing Siddhartha with distraction and giving him lessons in reading and writing, boxing, archery, and horseback riding, or having him make an inspection tour of the realm (Plates 2 and 3, lower left). Nothing helped. The next suggestion was that a marriage might have the power to divert him.

Life at the Court

Princess Gopi was the selected candidate. It was customary at that time that girls decided for themselves who they would marry. Gopi therefore organized a tournament and made it known that she would choose the one who excelled in courtly and military arts. Shuddhodana worried about this because the crown prince wasn't trained in anything. Nevertheless Siddhartha went to the competition in the company of his cousin Devadatta and half-brother Nanda and others.

An elephant had been placed inside the city gate to test who was the strongest. Devadatta killed the animal with one hand and Nanda pulled it to the side. Afterward Siddhartha showed up. He saw the senselessly killed animal, tossed it in an arc over the city wall, and the elephant instantly came to life again. At the tournament, the crown prince excelled in everything, including swimming and archery (Plates 3 and 4, lower left). Gopi picked him.

The marriage was consummated, but even this did not succeed in cheering Siddhartha up. A second marriage to two beauties, one of whom was Yashodhara, and countless concubines didn't kindle even a spark of joy in him. His every thought was focused on the road to salvation. At long last, it was decided to give the prince the opportunity of casting his gaze on the everyday world as it went about its business outside the palace walls.

The Four Encounters

The king proclaimed that the prince would ride out, and decreed that all the roads and towns were to look perfect and smell wonderful. The deities (remember, the deities at that time in Southern Asian history were Hindu deities) were of the opinion, however, that it was time that Sid-

Plate 2. The Life of the Buddha

dhartha should have his eyes opened and that he should give up his domestic situation for the salvation of humanity. This is why it was arranged that the crown prince would encounter aspects of life that had been unknown to him until then. For 29 years, Siddhartha had led a self-absorbed life of luxury at the court in Kapilavastu, largely ignorant of life outside the walls of his gilded cage. However, during some four trips he made with his horse and buggy outside the palace, he encountered people and phenomena that had remained hidden from him until that time. He came to the conclusion that the great majority of humanity lived in a far less carefree manner than he did. The average person led a hard, deplorable, and lamentable life. Due to samsara, there was little prospect for most people of an improved situation in their next earthly life.

He was forced to think after he saw an invalid, and learned from his driver that this aspect of life, although unfamiliar to him, was an everyday reality for a large part of the population. At the court, he was surrounded by young people and beauty, and the sight of an emaciated and sickly old man was a shock to him.

When he later saw a dead person being carried away, his servant told him that death awaits all of us, and that after rebirth most people return to another similarly miserable life.

During his fourth trip, he became aware of an ascetic beggar dressed in a saffron-colored robe, who moved from place to place apparently without worry, and who had withdrawn from everyday life in the hope of gaining spiritual understanding. Siddhartha wanted to arrive at a view for himself regarding the causes of human suffering. With the knowledge he hoped to gain, he had in mind formulating a system of salvation that would benefit not only his fellows, but humanity as a whole (these scenes are in different places, slightly to the right of center in Plates 2, 3, and 4; in Plate 1, all four are lower left, where the monk is depicted surrounded by an aureole).

On returning to the palace, he sunk into brooding thoughts and was even more cheerless than before. A minister advised the king to have the crown prince oversee farming operations. But when Siddhartha saw how ploughs tore the earth

open, churning up worms that were immediately eaten by birds, and how frogs were consumed by snakes, while peacocks polished off the snakes, and falcons dove down on the peacocks, he became sad at heart.

Siddhartha Secretly Leaves the Palace

Back at the palace, Siddhartha realized that at home, he would never find the solution to put an end to all suffering. That evening there was a big party, and after the bacchanalia, when everybody was asleep, Siddhartha snuck out of the palace (Plate 2, lower right; Plate 3, bottom, slightly to the left of center), and mounted his horse, Kanthaka. To prevent the hoof-beats from waking anyone, the gods lifted the horse up. Far outside the city, the prince said farewell to horse and servant. Sitting in front of a stupa (to the right, just below the center in all four examples), he cut off his long hair, removed his jewelry and expensive clothing, and wrapped himself in a simple monk's robe. Siddhartha was to study under various masters.

A stupa is a monument that is both connected with the death of Shakyamuni, and with death in general. The original dome-shaped earth mound resembles a burial mound that later evolved into the shapes seen in these thangkas to the right of center and in the upper right. Shakyamuni's cremains were kept here and worshipped here. Later, holy people in general were kept in these burial mounds. The stupa here is a portrayal of the symbolic death Siddhartha experienced when he "died to his first 29 years," to go out on his own.

Ascetism

After various experiences with wise teachers, Siddhartha had the feeling he wasn't getting anywhere. Along with five companions, he subjected himself to strict asceticism and self-denial (Plate 2, bottom, center; Plates 1 and 3, right, center). He limited his food intake to one sesame seed or one rice grain a day. After six years, although he was emaciated, he was not a step closer to the hoped-for understanding. Convinced that this extreme method did not result in ultimate understanding, he decided on another approach. He started eating again and went on by himself,

Plate 3. The Life of the Buddha

under reproach from his fellow ascetics, and found a quiet place where he hoped to meditate in silence. He stopped in Bodhgaya and sat down to think under a large fig or pipal tree (ficus religiosa, also called a bodhi tree or bo tree). A local grass cutter offered him a soft bundle of grass to sit on (Plate 3, right, center; actually this tableaux should be in the lower right.

The same goes for Plate 4; to the right sits a monkey offering food).

Mara's Attack

During his seven weeks of pondering and meditation, Mara, the personification of evil, tried to prevent Siddhartha from coming to the ultimate understanding. Mara sent his armies of monsters, but all their weapons and fired arrows transformed into flowers. As a final attack, Mara deployed his stunning, sensual daughters, who danced voluptuously around Siddhartha, and attempted to seduce him. Mara said that nobody would believe that he had not succumbed to their tricks and techniques. At this, the solitary Siddhartha called the earth goddess to be his witness, by signaling down with his right hand. The earth opened and the goddess confirmed that he had remained steadfast. Mara backed down and slunk away. In some traditions Mara's daughters are not brought into the picture until after Siddhartha attains Enlightenment (see Plates 1, 2, and 3, center and lower right).

Enlightenment

After 49 days of thinking and meditating, Siddhartha received insight into both his former and present lives. He came to the conclusion that extremes in life lead to nothing, that life is suffering, and that suffering must be eliminated. When he reached this insight, he attained nirvana, or liberation, enlightenment, or bodhi, and he, himself, became a Buddha, an Enlightened One, or, better yet, an Awakened One.

The title of "Buddha" for the historical person Siddhartha Gautama is incorrect, since anyone can become a buddha. It is better to speak of "the Buddha" when the enlightened Siddhartha is meant. He is, after all, the first person who attained enlightenment, and the article "the" dis-

tinguishes him from any others who might achieve enlightenment after him, and who would then also be buddhas.

It is good to realize that nirvana can be attained in full health and well-being. It is merely an indication of the fact that somebody has attained a stage where he (not she; for women there is also an opportunity for liberation, but first they have to be reborn as men in order to have a chance) has gathered so much wisdom and insight that rebirth after death will not take place again. Samsara, or the cycle of rebirth, will have been broken. Nirvana cannot be translated as Death (the Buddha lived another 45 years after his bodhi), or Nothing. It can be better described as Snuffing Out, Extinction, Deathlessness, No Longer Incarnatable.

The Buddha had experienced two extremes in his 35 years: on the one hand, 29 years of carefree life at the court, a life of extravagant luxury and excessive (sensual) pleasure, full of "wine, women, and song," and, on the other, his six years of asceticism. Neither extreme led to understanding. The Buddha formulated the teaching of the Four Noble Truths. The focus here is the Middle Way:

1) Life is suffering. This is evident. Most people lead a life of woe. Illness and poverty dominate most people's lives.
2) Why is life suffering? This is because people are too attached to certain attainments and forms of pleasure. One person's pleasure is gained at another's expense. Therefore people burden themselves with negative karma and consequently the cycle of rebirth simply continues.
3) Suffering must stop. If people don't change their way of living, samsara will continue. Only changing patterns of behavior will lead to the cessation of suffering.
4) How can suffering be eliminated? To this end, the Buddha formulated the Noble Eightfold Path: right understanding, right intention, right speech, right action, right way of living, right concentration, right effort, right mindfulness. The Eightfold Path is at the core of his teachings and forms the point of departure for all kinds of interpretations. The human being lies at the center of all the

Plate 4. The Life of the Buddha

Buddha's thought and action. He does not recognize a concept like God or Creator, thus no Higher or Absolute Being.

After another period of seven weeks during which the Buddha sat, meditated, and walked, he contemplated the consequences of the fact that he had attained nirvana and what he should do with this knowledge. He decided to make his understanding known.

Proclaiming the Teachings

The Buddha walked from Bodhgaya to Varanasi (Benares), the largest and most thriving city in the region. It was ruled by a king and there was a generous group of patrons in the form of well-to-do nobility and the upper middle class. He went to preach in nearby Sarnath, in the deer park, or rather, "He set the wheel (chakra) of teachings (dharma) into motion."

Here he met his five former fellow ascetics. They noticed the unusual glow that the Buddha radiated. After their initial skepticism, they listened to his words. Their leader summarized the dharma with the words: all that exists will pass away. They were the first to join the Buddha and they formed the beginning of the monastic order (Plate 2, upper right). For the next 45 years Shakyamuni journeyed throughout Northern India with his followers and announced the message of salvation. During the monsoons, the group would stay in gardens and buildings, monasteries, that had been donated by well-to-do supporters.

Keep in mind that Shakyamuni, the honorific title he received by virtue of his wisdom, was and remained a Hindu. He was, however, a Hindu who was to formulate a method of escape from the vicious cycle of rebirth. There is an opportunity, it's true, for a Hindu to realize *moksha*, or liberation, so that reincarnation will no longer occur, but the chance of succeeding is negligibly small. The power of the Buddha was that Shakyamuni formulated his teachings in simple terms and presented them without discrimination, negating caste differences.

In contrast to Hinduism, he turned against burnt offerings and animal sacrifices. His revulsion to the suffering of animals developed into ahimsa. This concept is one of the key points of the contemporary teaching of liberation in Jainism and became known again through Mahatma Gandhi. Later, Hinduism incorporated ahimsa in its own philosophy. Shakyamuni also thought the ritual bath was absurd as a method of getting rid of sins. Although he didn't condemn the caste system, he himself did not distinguish ancestry or native group; everyone was welcome and was treated equally.

Extraordinary Events

During his years of wandering, Buddha met with jealousy and suspicion as well as approval. In order to convince others of his holiness, sometimes he performed miracles. He transformed snake poison into flowers, and, in a fast-flowing river, he created a passage so he could cross and stay dry. Two important major events were his visit to his family and acquaintances in Kapilavastu, where he converted his father, and his journey to the Heaven of 33 gods. In this Trayastrimsha Heaven he taught Queen Maya, his mother. We see the Buddha seated on the throne of Indra, the king of the gods. He is sitting in the so-called European position, with his legs hanging down. By way of a ladder with 33 rungs, the Buddha descended to Earth. Usually this is represented by three little ladders side by side, each having eleven rungs (Plates 2, 3, and 4, upper right). Shakyamuni did not want to be glorified, saying that all he had done was to find a universal truth that is independent of any particular person. Nor did he want to create a religion—just a monastic order of individuals who had to find salvation for themselves. His comment, "As the sea is permeated with but one taste, salt, so are my words steeped in but one taste, liberation," is telling.

Parinirvana

At the age of 80, the Buddha died in Kushinagara. He attained parinirvana, which means definite nirvana, the passing beyond nirvana. His body was cremated, and the ashes and few unburned parts were divided into eight portions and placed in eight stupas.

In Plates 1 and 3, the moment of death, at which the Buddha was lying on his right side, has been depicted in the center, just below the large central scene where the Buddha is sitting on the throne. Fortified by his last words, the monastic order went on alone: "Be a lamp for yourself, be a refuge for yourself, seek no refuge outside yourself."

Buddhism became truly popular starting 250 years before our era, when it was able to count on the support of the Emperor Ashoka. Ashoka had the eight stupas opened and divided the remains among 84,000 stupas (the number 84,000 appears in many legends and should be taken with a grain of salt). It was also around this time that it was decided to put the teachings into writing. This canon was called the *tripitaka*, literally "the three baskets," as the collected texts were kept in three baskets. The tripitaka contains dogmatic work, with rules for monastic life, sutras (sermons), and jatakas (stories about the Buddha's previous lives).

In all four of these thangkas, the center is occupied by Shakyamuni Buddha. On his head the fontanel bulge, or ushnisha—-later interpreted as his extra mental capacity, in spite of its rather prosaic origin from his hair (which members of higher castes wore long)—-is tied up on his head and given extra emphasis here with a gold jewel shape. His long earlobes hearken back to his time as prince, when he was in the habit of wearing heavy gold discs in his ears, causing the lobes to stretch.

At the very top there is a small dark-blue naked buddha figure with a lady on his lap. This is the Adi Buddha, Samantabhadra, with his prajna (see page 22). Blue or blue-black is the color of the firmament, of the cosmic emptiness, *shunyata*.

III / Theravada Buddhism

Original Buddhism is called Theravada, the Doctrine of the Elders. In Theravada Buddhism people seek their own, individual nirvana. So it is ego-oriented, although one may be coached by teachings and have a teacher who provides explanation. Anyone following the path to its end and who becomes blessed with liberation is called an *arhat* (see Plates 12 and 13 on pages 33 and 36). Someone who has done this entirely alone and who has attained it only for himself is called a *pratyeka buddha*.

Essential to the continuity of Buddhist teaching is the triratna, the Three Jewels. They are:

1) *The Buddha—the initiator and inspiring example;*
2) *The dharma—the teachings;*
3) *The sangha—the congregation, the monastic community.*

Monks (there are also convents for nuns) are expected to be prepared to live according to the Eightfold Path and to break through samsara. A good layperson will stick to the five commandments (not to kill, not to steal, self-control, friendliness, and compassion) and will not yet strive for liberation, but will strive for a higher incarnation in hopes of finally becoming a monk through a series of increasingly better births. Only monks live purely and unsulliedly enough that they have a chance to break through samsara.

Monks ensure the continuance of the dharma with their monastic orders. Shariputra and Maudgalyayana, shown in Plate 5 on page 19, are symbols of the sangha, the monastic community.

Shakyamuni Buddha with Shariputra and Maudgalyayana

When Mara's evil forces attacked Siddhartha while he was in meditation under the pipal tree in Bodhgaya, with a motion of his right hand, he called the earth to bear witness to the fact that he had not succumbed to Mara's ruses and wiles. This hand position is shown in Plate 5; the Buddha's right hand, resting on the right knee, fingertips touching the earth, is in what is called *bhu-misparshamudra*. This mudra appears most often in thangkas portraying the Buddha. The mere sight of this mudra guarantees the believer that it will ward off all evil. His left hand is resting palm upward on his legs, which are folded in the meditation position with bare feet sole upward.

In the palm of his left hand lies a beggar's cup, the attribute of all Theravada Buddhist monks who pass by houses in the morning to beg for food. The monks are to accept the food that is given them, including meat. Around noon, all the monks eat the food together as the only meal of the day. This practice still occurs in countries like Burma and Thailand where Theravada Buddhism is prominent. The beggar's cup is a standard attribute of Amitabha, Shakyamuni, and Bhaisajyaguru.

Aside from the position of hands and feet, there are five more characteristic physical hallmarks which a meditator must possess: a straight back, straight shoulders, eyes focused on the end of the nose, lips and jaw in a naturally relaxed position, while the tip of the tongue touches the roof of the mouth, and the chin is positioned at the height of the Adam's apple, from an onlooker's point of view.

A monk's original, simple, cotton clothing comprises a wrap for the lower body, one for the upper body, and another to cloak the upper torso. As can be seen from monks in many orders in various countries, this dress requirement is still fully honored in practice. Only in the art of painting has clothing become much more "chic."

The Buddha sits under a parasol, a symbol that, on the one hand, indicates an important personage, such as a king or an important spiritual leader, and on the other, offers protection from unknown potential dangers. A parasol is one of the eight tokens of good luck (see Plate 7 on page 25).

The Buddha had a number of favorite students. One was his cousin Ananda who appears frequently in Sri Lanka's Theravada Buddhism. Ananda was well-loved and extremely popular because of his gentle character, and because he treated women as fully worthy, for he instructed

Plate 5. Shakyamuni Buddha with Shariputra and Maudgalyayana

nuns. The Buddha was far ahead of his time, but also a product of his time, in that he did not consider women inferior, but only reluctantly agreed to allow women into the order.

The two disciples we encounter everywhere in northern Buddhism are Shariputra and Maudgalyayana. They stand, from the Buddha's perspective, to the right and left of his throne, each holding an alms bowl and a jingling beggar's staff. In the thangka they radiate holiness, with their nimbuses, which are green here, and a transparent *mandorla* glowing behind each of them. They stand in an opulent green landscape, each on a little square rug.

Both were sons of Brahmans. They met at a party where everybody was singing, dancing, and having fun. They were the only ones to disregard these amusements. They decided to withdraw from social interaction to become monks and seek perfection. They met a wise old man, a teacher who had a lot of knowledge, but who also knew that true perfection would be taught when a wise member of the Shakya decided to become a monk. He advised them to seek their salvation in the future with him. And so it came to pass. Maudgalyayana asked whether Shariputra, the smarter of the two (that is also why he stands on the Buddha's right, because right is better than left), would share his knowledge with him if he were to gain understanding first. Each promised to help the other. They were informed as to where they could meet the Buddha, "that deep ocean of wisdom, in the transforming effect of whose immaculacy they would be able to bathe." Just before they did, however, they met a false holy man. He was afraid that he would lose his many followers to the new way of thinking. He whis-

pered bad things about their inspiring new teacher, but they saw through his treachery. They reached the wisest of the Shakya, and requested to be admitted into the monastic order. As soon as the Buddha had agreed to this, their hair spontaneously fell out, and they took a metaphorical bath in the deep sea of immaculacy.

Eventually, they became his best students. In hopes of helping sinners gain a better rebirth and thereby offering them the possibility of a virtuous life, they descended into hell. There, numerous people were paying dreadful penance for their sins, including Shakyamuni's grudge-bearing cousin, Devadatta. Shariputra was known for his sharp, analytical ability, and Maudgalyayana excelled in clairvoyance and magical powers.

Because they could not bear the thought of dying after the Buddha, he allowed them to depart the world sooner, both on the same day in the year 486 b.c.e. Shariputra died first, and Maudgalyayana, who is also sometimes called Mahamaudgalyayana (*maha* means "great"), in the afternoon. There are traditions that claim that Maudgalyayana was murdered near Rajgir by religious opponents.

While Ananda was associated in later times with popular beliefs, the philosophical and dialectical Shariputra was connected with Mahayana Buddhism, and the mediumistic and mystically oriented Maudgalyayana with Tantric Buddhism. The rich robes they wear are actually not worthy of a monk. In later times, when Mahayana Buddhism became prevalent, the desire for luxury and comfort grew. In thangka paintings silk, gold thread, and brocade are considered to be tokens of honor.

IV / Mahayana Buddhism

Around the beginning of our era, a reformation took place, because, for many people, the path to salvation turned out to be too hard in the long run, even for monks. This new trend is referred to as Mahayana to distinguish it from the previous trend that is disparagingly called Hinayana. *Mahayana* literally means "the great path," or "great vehicle," while *Hinayana* means "the lesser path." Followers of Mahayana considered their school of thought better or greater than original Buddhism, which has the more neutral and friendly name of Theravada, "Doctrine of the Elders." Mahayana was deemed better because more people were able to benefit from this method of salvation.

Aside from the Eightfold Path, the new direction included more roads to liberation, the return of the divine element, and the alluring prospect of a heavenly paradise.

In contrast to ego-oriented Theravada Buddhism, with its pratyeka buddhas and arhats, in fellow-human-oriented Mahayana Buddhism, divine helpers, or *bodhisattvas*, appear on the path to liberation. A bodhisattva is a being (*sattva*) who has reached enlightenment (*bodhi*), or nirvana, but who delays entry into parinirvana out of compassion for muddleheaded humanity. As long as there is suffering, bodhisattvas will remain.

Bodhisattvas help people and guide the deceased to heaven. The idea of various heavens, seen as pure countries and "places to park" until the moment of reincarnation came, grew in Mahayana Buddhism. Amitabha Buddha's Sukhavati heaven became extremely popular. In the end, though, the ultimate goal is still to break through samsara, not to end up in heaven.

Mahayana Buddhism allows the divine element to return. The Buddha, who did not recognize a divine creator and who did not want to be worshipped, was honored and venerated as a teacher for 500 years. In art, for reasons of respect, he was indicated only by symbols. However, in the first century of our era the buddha image was introduced. Then, for several centuries, the Buddha, with or without an escort of bodhisattvas, was the main focus of veneration. Some centuries later, a whole pantheon emerged in which the historical Buddha was only one of many buddhas.

The combination of rebirth in a Buddhist paradise and a world of deities that can be worshipped shows a parallel with the practice of Hinduism. In Hinduism at about this time, the bhakti movement began to develop whereby people approached the deity through individual rituals. For the bulk of the people, an eternal, omnipotent Buddha, who guarded over the universe and humanity, was attractive. The Buddha became a being worthy of worship, a god.

Mahayana Buddhism, which was less elite than Theravada Buddhism, provided more opportunity for popular belief. Prayer was directed at buddhas, bodhisattvas, and other deities, with appeals for health, fertility, a good harvest, many children, money, and entreaties to remain protected from natural disasters, epidemics, and snakebites.

Theravada Buddhism, in fact, also recognizes a bodhisattva, namely Maitreya, the Buddha of the Future who is, technically speaking, still a bodhisattva. The most popular bodhisattva in Mahayana Buddhism is Avalokiteshvara, the merciful lord who, filled with compassion, gazes down on humanity. In addition, Manjushri and Vajrapani appear frequently.

Mahayana monasteries remained in existence, but were moved to quieter places often located far away from the busy cities. The monks no longer lived at begging distance. The people periodically came to the monasteries with donations. By necessity, these would also include material things, because food is perishable, and so began a monetary economy in the monastic world. Gradually, various monasteries became large landowners, with personnel that worked the land for pay, or sometimes partially for free because this was good for one's karma. And so luxuries like jewelry, silk robes, and changes in the concept of celibacy crept into the monastic life as well.

In Mahayana Buddhism, the idea developed that Shakyamuni was the last, up to that point, in a series of buddhas. The series recommences with Maitreya, who is therefore called the Buddha of the Future. The most common system of dividing periods of time is based on the number five; Mahayana Buddhism enumerates five eras of human existence on Earth. Three of them lie behind us. We are living in the fourth period, in which Shakyamuni was born as an earthly buddha, and 5,000 years after his death the fifth period of the world will begin with Maitreya as buddha.

There are two kinds of bodhisattvas. There are mortals who want to achieve buddhahood, and who help others through their knowledge of and will to enlightenment (*bodhicitta*). There are also active projections—emanations of a buddha—and thus "divine" beings. Both, however, embody the bodhicitta, and both exist to help people. In a later development, the bodhicitta was considered to be latent in every person, like a seed. In Tantric Buddhism, a person can either concentrate on this divine seed inside the body and cultivate it, or else merge with it.

The idea of multiple buddhas and bodhisattvas prompted a systemizing of their functions and appearances. This led, in Mahayana Buddhism, to the difficult concept of the *trikaya*, which literally means "three bodies," and which concerns three realms or levels in which or on which a buddha manifests.

The point of departure here is an invisible, intangible, and self-created primeval Buddha, or Adi Buddha (a concept comparable to the absolutely divine Brahman of the Hindus). The invisible and formless Adi Buddha sojourns passively in the nirvana or shunyata state "in the heights," or in a lofty, heavenly realm. He is the equivalent of his teachings, dharma, and exists as such in *dharmakaya* (kaya means "body").

While it is difficult to impart visual form to something invisible, the Adi Buddha has a recognizable appearance in art. He is portrayed as a white or dark-blue buddha with both crown and jewels. Depending on the monastic order or school, the Adi Buddha may have different attire and names, such as Vajradhara, Vajrasattva, Vajrapani, Mahavairocana, or Samantabhadra. Only Samantabhadra is naked and wears no accessories. (There also happens to be a bodhisattva, Samantabhadra, who should not be confused with the Adi Buddha of the same name.) The Adi Buddha sits in *dhyanasana*, the meditation position, alone or with a female partner (see Plates 2, 3, and 4 on pages 11 and 15).

Out of the Adi Buddha's permanent state of meditation, the Five Dhyani Buddhas emanate in a spiritual sense. These five are located in a lower cosmic realm (*sambhogakaya*). They are the component factors of the all-encompassing wisdom of the Adi Buddha. By meditating on a dhyani buddha and identifying with it, the believer will become familiar with one part of the ur-Buddha.

Dhyani buddha means "meditation buddha." Another term is *jina*, meaning "messiah" or "victor" in the spiritual realm. A third term is *tathagata*, which means "the one who came," "the one who made it." The term tathagata is confusing because it is also used as an honorific title for Shakyamuni who, hierarchically, is on an earthly, or lower, level than the jinas.

The dhyani buddhas are mystical extensions of the Adi Buddha and invisible. However, they, too, are given form, namely as buddha figures. If a dhyani buddha preaches to his bodhisattvas, he is attired as a lord. When not preaching, he is dressed in normal monk's robes, without accessories. *Sambhoga* means enjoyment, satisfaction, splendor. This description should be viewed in the sense that the listeners, in the case of the bodhisattvas, are enjoying and deriving satisfaction from the splendor of the preaching dhyani buddha.

The five dhyani buddhas are Vairocana, Akshobhya, Ratnasambhava, Amitabha, and Amoghasiddhi associated with the directions center, east, south, west, and north respectively, and each has a color: white; blue; yellow; red; and green. Each one also has specific mudras, attributes, elements, and numerous other telltale signs.

Plate 6. The Buddha with Dhyani Buddhas

This quintuple system is the most current, but there are also other systems with six or seven periods of the world, and six or seven dhyani buddhas.

The Buddha with Dhyani Buddhas

The thangka in Plate 6, page 23, is an example of the freedom of the modern-day painter. In the center, in nothing like a simple monk's robe, sits the manushi buddha, Shakyamuni. Dhyani buddhas have been depicted all around, but are not unduly consistent. The green Amoghasiddhi has been given the hand position called abhayamudra ("Have No Fear" mudra, a raised hand with open palm forward), the blue Akshobhya is in bhumisparshamudra ("Calling the Earth to Bear Witness" mudra), the red Amitabha is sitting in dhyanamudra ("Meditation" mudra), and white Vairocana is in dharmachakramudra ("Setting the Wheel of Teachings into Motion" mudra). These four have been portrayed according to the rules, but the yellow Ratnasambhava, with his varamudra ("Giving or Granting" mudra), is missing, and Vairocana appears twice and Akshobhya three times.

On a tangible level, dhyani bodhisattvas—also simply called bodhisattvas—sojourn in the same sambhogakaya. They form the accessible connecting links, approachable through prayer, between the worshipper and the dhyani buddha. Direct help can be expected from a bodhisattva in areas such as the path that one has to walk to achieve enlightenment.

Since bodhisattvas are neither monks nor buddhas, and so still stand with both feet planted in earthly life, they are dressed in expensive robes and adorned with jewelry. Mind you, art usually stands apart from theology. This is why, in thangkas, the Buddha is inevitably painted in noble attire.

On a still more directly approachable level, namely the earth plane (*nirmanakaya, nirmana* meaning "physical presence" or "physical appearance"), lives a manushi buddha. A manushi buddha, who is supposed to be clothed as a monk, is a human, and so a mortal incarnation of a bodhisattva.

Where a manushi buddha incarnates only for the duration of a single human lifetime, his bodhisattva's "length of rule" is an entire period of the world, which at the present time is 5,000 years. A bodhisattva may have several incarnations during one world period.

From this it follows that the historical individual who stood at the beginning of the teaching of liberation that we call Buddhism—-Siddhartha the person—-figures a lot less prominently in later Mahayana Buddhism than in Theravada Buddhism. He is but a part of a series, and worship of him by the believer does not automatically lead to the ultimate goal, nirvana.

For example, the fourth or current period of the world has Amitabha as its dhyani buddha, whose color is red and whose hands are in dhyanamudra, lying on top of each other in his lap, palms upward. His bodhisattva is Avalokiteshvara, who appears in many guises, but he always wears a small figurine of his spiritual father, Amitabha, in his crown or hair. The earthly buddha who belongs here is Shakyamuni.

The Series of Buddhas

At his birth, Siddhartha said that he was coming to earth for the last time and this was the last in a perpetual series of existences. The many previous existences of the Buddha are known from legends and jatakas, stories about his previous births. In Mahayana Buddhism, the idea developed that the historic Buddha was only one in a long series of buddhas. Shakyamuni's period will last 5,000 years, until about the year 4500, after which the new buddha, Maitreya, will come.

In the later forms of Buddhism, the theology grew and, incidentally, so did the number of buddhas, to a series of 8, 9, 24, 35, 52, or 1,000, and various other numbers. Here, it is not the power of the story that counts, but the might of the number, with its symbolic value of infinity. Much is good, more is better, or there strength in numbers and repetition. In fact, it is a theological impoverishment, caused by many teachers.

This type of portrayal is typical in monasteries with what are known as thousand-buddha walls, and they frequently appear as a thangka theme.

Plate 7. Series of Buddhas

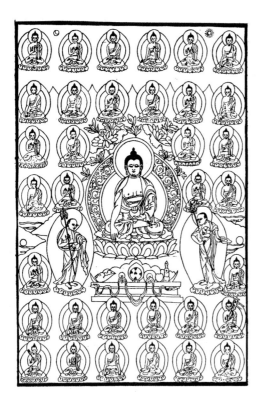

Figure 6. Block print of the 35 Confessional Buddhas

Figure 7. Block print of the Eight Medicine Buddhas

The positive effect of this numerousness is equal to the endless circling of a prayer wheel that contains a mantra such as OM MANI PADME HUM, and which people turn, repeating the prayer over and over.

The thangka in Plate 7 (p. 25) most closely resembles a thousand-buddha wall. The central buddha, Shakyamuni, is sitting in bhumisparshamudra and is repeated over and over, in identical fashion, in a long series.

Below his throne, and between Shariputra and Maudgalyayana, the intertwined form of the frequently occurring symbol of fortune, *ashtamangala*, the eight good luck tokens, can be seen. Although odd numbers are more positive than even numbers, eight is still one of the lucky numbers (consider, among other things, the eight cardinal directions, the Eightfold Path). The ashtamangala consists of:

Parasol

First and foremost the parasol offers protection from rain and sun. Out of this grew its function as status symbol: important personages, deities, and the Buddha have the right to a parasol. In a religious sense, a parasol offers protection from unfavorable influences and symbolizes spiritual power.

Fish

Originally, fish were a symbol of the Ganges and Yamuna Rivers in Northern India. Later, they represented water in general, and, by association, fertility, prosperity, and happiness.

Treasure Pot

A pot contains water or food. It conveys the idea of gratifying physical needs. Out of this grew the ideal of a pot that is never empty, or a symbol of wish fulfillment (spiritual and material).

Lotus

A lotus is born in the mud, finds its way upward, and opens just above the surface of the water in all spotlessness. It is a symbol of immaculacy, of the spirit that is. (the lotus doesn't grow in Tibet, so it is often highly stylized in thangkas.)

Plate 8. Series of Buddhas

Conch shell

The white, right-turning (left is more common in nature, but right is more positive than left) whelk is associated with water, and is used on altars for, among other things, incense offerings. Priests also blow on conchs, therefore it is a symbol of the Buddha's fame because the sound of the trumpet goes in all directions.

Wheel

The chakra was once a disk-shaped weapon and sun symbol. The spokes of the wheel symbolize the eight compass points. It is the signature symbol of Buddhism. In Sarnath, the Buddha set the wheel in motion; his teachings began to gain momentum.

Shrivatsa

This is the perpetual knot, with neither beginning nor end; everything is interconnected. It is a symbol of the infinity of Buddhism.

Banner

As a sign of victory, this is the symbol of compassionate Buddhist knowledge winning out over ignorance.

The thangka in Plate 8 (on page 27) is typologically comparable to the one in Plate 7 (on page 25). The number of buddhas is not known to be of a standard series. In this painting the repetition is somewhat less monotonous than in the previous one, because a little variation has been introduced in the hand positions. This thangka was done in red with gold detail, a type of thangka that is used for friendly or protective deities.

The thangka in Plate 9, on page 29, shows a variation on a well-known theme. A frequently occurring series is the 35 Confessional Buddhas, with the Buddha, Shakyamuni, in the middle, and around him 34 of his component factors. Beside his throne stand Shariputra and Maudgalyayana. Buddhism recognizes 35 serious violations and sins against the teachings. The sinner who repents will find for each misstep a buddha who will point the way to a better attitude toward life. All 35 have a name. They only appear in the specific context of the Confessional Buddha. Numerologists have given the number 35 a cosmic dimension by breaking it down into the four cardinal directions and the four intermediary directions plus zenith and nadir, and the axis between, as well as the 24 vertical intermediary divisions. Thus explained, the number 35 expresses the omnipresence of the Buddha. In this thangka the painter largely followed the layout but did not stick to the proper number. The same attitude is evident in the Tibetan writing at the bottom which suggests more than it tells. From a technical perspective this thangka is a variation on a gold thangka.

Depicted at the bottom, in the center, is Nagarjuna, the Southern Indian scholar from the second century c.e., who formulated the madhyamika (the Middle Way) and who is considered a great theoretician of Mahayana Buddhism. Nagarjuna can be recognized by the snake's hood above his head. Nagarjuna's madhyamika relies on the dualistic view of being and non-being, and is strongly based on the *Prajnaparamita*, the Sutra of Transcendental Wisdom. Later the *Prajnaparamita* is personified as a goddess because in Buddhism *prajna*, or "wisdom," is seen as a feminine characteristic.

In the 14th century, Nagarjuna's philosophy would form the basis of the Yellow Hat Order. The second great Mahayana philosophy which would continue through Vajrayana Buddhism, is the Yogacara School, developed between the third and fifth centuries, based on yoga and meditation.

Medicine Buddhas

The point of departure and core of the Buddha's thought is his teaching on suffering. Human suffering must be eliminated. The Buddha can be seen as a physician because he diagnosed suffering and developed his teachings on liberation, or dharma, as medicine to escape from the cycle of rebirth. He also saw himself as a physician, namely one who immediately healed the wound, in view of the patient, by asking about the cause of the injury.

Those for whom this highly cerebral level is a step too far would sooner think to call on the Buddha to heal physical ailments. This concept

Plate 9. Series of Buddhas

developed particularly in Tibet. Tibet owed much of its medical knowledge to texts from India. Thus, the science of Ayurvedic medicine also reached the Himalayas. Considering this knowledge was not specifically Buddhist, although it did accompany Buddhist teaching, a buddha was created, along the analogy of Shakyamuni as spiritual healer, who symbolized medicinal knowledge. This system was expanded to the Eight Medicine Buddhas. Of these eight, Bhaisajyaguru is the most important exponent. He attained great popularity and is the only one who is depicted by himself without the other seven. In popular belief, looking at or touching a thangka of medicine buddhas has a curative effect.

Bhaisajyaguru

Plate 10 depicts Bhaisajyaguru in his characteristic body color, blue. Possibly, this color is connected with his title, Lord of the Lapis Lazuli-Colored Light. Ground gemstones were ingredients in medications, so, no doubt, was expensive blue lapis, as well. Bhaisajyaguru means "Supreme Healer," "the Lord Who Has a Healing Effect."

He rests his left hand on his lap, and his upwardly-opened palm holds a beggar's bowl. In the bowl lies a fruit from the healing herb he is holding in his right hand. The plant is a myrobalan plum, a variety that is used as a laxative, or purgative.

The symmetrical presentation is situated in a fantasy landscape where animals range peaceably. In the foreground are some good luck symbols.

When the eight medicine buddhas are depicted together, they are either grouped around the blue Bhaisajyaguru or the gold colored Shakyamuni, the supreme physician.

A Medicinal Thangka

A variation on this last theme can be seen in the thangka in Plate 11, page 32. Depicted in the center is Bhaisajyaguru. But instead of the seven other medicine buddhas, there are four buddha figures grouped around him, sitting on the four cardinal directions as if they were dhyani buddhas. The rest of the painting has been executed as a homeopathic *materia medica*. The descriptions of the plants are written in Tibetan underneath.

Ancient Indian medicine, is explained in the Ayurveda, a series of native Indian medicinal books, of which the oldest dates from around the fifth century b.c.e. Tibetan medicine is based on a Tibetan handbook from the eighth century c.e. that makes use of native knowledge of the healing effects of plants and minerals, combined with Chinese and Ayurvedic principles.

Illness occurs when the balance among the three bodily fluids comprising the human—air, bile, and mucus—is disturbed. Such a disturbance can arise when there is an imbalance in the component parts of the fluids, the five elements of earth, water, fire, air, and ether (prana).

In the Buddhist sense, hatred, wanting (desire), and ignorance (stupidity) are the main ailments that torment and poison the body and soul (see the Bhavachakra, Plates 27 and 28 on pages 65, and 67). They disturb the balance of bodily fluids so that illness arises. There are also external influences at work that can negatively impact the body, such as evil spirits, a particular position of the planets, negative karma, improper food, and irreligious behavior. The religious cure is right thinking and acting. Calling on particular deities and meditation may be part of the therapy.

Tibetan healthcare comprises a combination of somatic and psycho-philosophical healing. In regard to the former healing method, the doctor will give nutritional advice and administer pills made from minerals and herbs. There are dozens of combinations of different plant extracts. Animal parts too, such as snakeskin, processed reptiles, ground tiger bone or rhinoceros horn, might be part of the medication, albeit in smaller quantities than plants and minerals, partly in view of the price.

A series of medicinal plants may appear not just in thangkas but also in monasteries in the form of large murals (see figure 8, page 34).

The Medicine Buddha

The medicine buddha portrayed in the center of Plate 12, page 33, is absolutely in keeping with the previous two. Still, it seems as if Bhaisajyaguru is supposed to be seen here as a direct emanation of

Plate 10. Bhaisajyaguru, the Medicine Buddha

Plate 11. Medicinal Thangka

Plate 12. Medicine Buddha

Figure 8. Monastery entrance with painting of medicinal trees and plants

Shakyamuni Buddha. The Buddha is seated in lavish robes on a no less lavish throne, in front of which stands a low table, done in the Chinese style, with a number of lucky charms and precious things on it. On the two white panels of the throne, peacocks have been painted. Peacocks, like eagles, are the enemies of poisonous snakes, which they like to kill. They are also capable of eating poisonous plants without being affected. Ground peacock feathers are reputed to be an antidote to snake poison. The peacocks can be interpreted in the medicinal context of this thangka. Human ignorance should be seen as a toxin for which the Buddha's teachings are the remedy. The medicine buddha is flanked by two bodhisattvas with red nimbuses. To the left is Suryaprabha (he often holds a sword, like Manjushri; here the painter has portrayed Manjushri's other attribute, a book), and to the right, Chandraprabha, who often wears a moon-shaped piece of jewelry. Suryaprabha's and Chandaprabha's names mean "Sunlight" and "Moonlight." Both are standing in what is considered to be a highly aesthetic position, the *tribhanga* position, which originated in India, whereby the body makes two sharp bends, and so forms three axes on top of one another. The five dhyani buddhas are seated on lotus pillows, hovering in the clouds above the medicine buddha. They can be recognized more readily by their body colors than by their hand positions.

Somewhat behind the throne sit two monks, their heads shaven. Both are sitting on little rugs that have been rendered in the Indian style, i.e. with an improper perspective. Normally a rectangular object on a flat plane exhibits converging lines. The lines on the sides, if they were traced further, would join at a single point. Indian painting of recent centuries, however, except that of Mughal, has allowed the lines to diverge. More interesting is the question of who is sitting on the little rugs. Both figures can clearly be deduced to be arhats.

Arhats are historical persons among the followers of the Buddha. They form a group of sixteen disciples who were selected by him, on the basis of their knowledge and experience in achieving nirvana, to remain on Earth and to protect the teachings as long as the dharma existed. This is equivalent to a period of 5,000 years, until the coming of the next Buddha. *Arhat* means "Venerable One," and is the name for someone who is wise and holy, who during life attained nirvana.

The presence of two arhats in this thangka is entirely in line with how they are venerated. According to tradition, the King of Kham, Eastern Tibet, was extremely ill once, and no therapy was working. Offerings and prayers to the arhats led to his recovery.

The arhat to the left of the Buddha is Bakula, the oldest of the sixteen. He became 70 before the birth of Shakyamuni as the son of a Brahman. After the death of his parents, Bakula became an ascetic and withdrew into the wilderness. The fruits of the fields made up his diet, his clothing consisted of bark; Bakula is also the name of a kind of tree. At an advanced age, he became a disciple of the Buddha, and attained nirvana. Due to his ascetic way of life, he suffered no illnesses for 160 years.

Bakula remembered all his former lives. He had been a seller of medicines once, ages before. And on another occasion he had distributed arura, the same plum-like fruit that Bhaisajyaguru holds. Thus, he obviously has a connection with medicine. The little animal he is holding in his hand is a nakula, a mongoose (see Plate 37, page 87). It is associated with treasure and wealth. In this case, it points to spiritual treasure and intellectual wealth.

The arhat to the right of the Buddha is Rahula-bhadra, the son of Siddhartha and Yashodhara, who was conceived on the evening of the Great Exodus from the palace. On the same day that Siddhartha attained enlightenment, six years later, his son Rahula was born, ending Yashodhara's extremely long pregnancy. When Rahula turned 6, the Buddha visited the palace for a day. The boy followed him and was later initiated by Shariputra. On his deathbed, the Buddha asked his son to remain on earth as an arhat along with the fifteen others.

Various versions of this story run contrary to one another. On the one hand, it is said that Rahula was already born when the Buddha left the palace. On the other hand, there are traditions in which Rahula was just a good student who excelled at little and that he died long before his father. This would still make him an arhat, but not one of the sixteen.

The attribute by which Rahula can be recognized is a gold crown. The arhat obtained it when he went to the Heaven of the 33 Gods to ask for alms. Meanwhile, he converted many of the deities' children, who gave him their gold head-dresses in gratitude. Rahula made one crown out of the many.

Directly below the throne of the medicine buddha sits the Green Tara. Below her, slightly to the left, sits a worshipper, and behind his back, a scantily clad man is about to fall into a gorge; he is possibly a symbol of somebody who has lost his way in a spiritual sense and needs to be cured of his erring. The bottom edge reveals symbols of longevity derived from Chinese iconography, such as deer, rocks, and an evergreen. Lying in bowls are symbols of good luck, including a number of the Seven Jewels (a king's and queen's earrings, coral, elephant tusks), and pearls and peaches, which are often used in medicine.

The little, blue, thickset figure in the lower right looks a bit like a daka. A *daka* ("eater") is a kind of *yaksha*, an earth spirit who devours whatever is bad for humans. A daka is portrayed as a scantily clad gnome, usually with an open mouth.

There are hollow statuettes of dakas, whose mouths are used to administer medications to patients. The figure depicted here, however, is fashionably dressed and holds a nakula in one hand, elements which, when taken together with his stout build, point to Jambhala. Instead of Jambhala's customary jambhara fruit—a kind of lemon—in his other hand he is holding an object that derives from Chinese art. It strongly resembles a *ju-i*, a scepter with the symbolic value of happiness and prosperity. This scepter derives from the mystical long-life mushroom, a variety of mushroom that is considered to confer longevity and, when consumed in large quantities, eternal life. The trilobed end of the ju-i, executed in the lucky color red, has the shape of a flying bat, another Chinese symbol of good fortune and longevity, and an animal whose various parts are processed in medications.

The Eighteen Arhats

At first glance, the Chinese quality of the thangka in Plate 13, on page 36, is striking. Robes, water, clouds, and animals have been rendered in the Chinese style. This is not an accident. Outside of the central medallion, which includes the Buddha and a few acolytes, with a ship down to the right and a man with a tiger down to the left, there are seven groups containing from one to six identically clad monks. These are the arhats who are on their way to China. They were invited by the Chinese emperor to teach an intensive summer course in Buddhism. The sixteen can be individually recognized by standard attributes, such as an incense burner, a fly whisk, a miniature stupa, a book, a glowing gem, or a string of jewels.

Veneration of the sixteen arhats originated in India and became extremely popular in China and Tibet. In both countries they also appear as a group of eighteen, and in China, where they are known as the Lohan, their number later grew to five hundred. In fact, in Tibet, they function as bodhisattvas in their role of helpers on the path to enlightenment. They travel all over the world to perform their task properly, and may wear the clothing of the country in which they are sojourning.

Tibetan painting was primarily influenced by India, but after the 17th century, it derived a lot

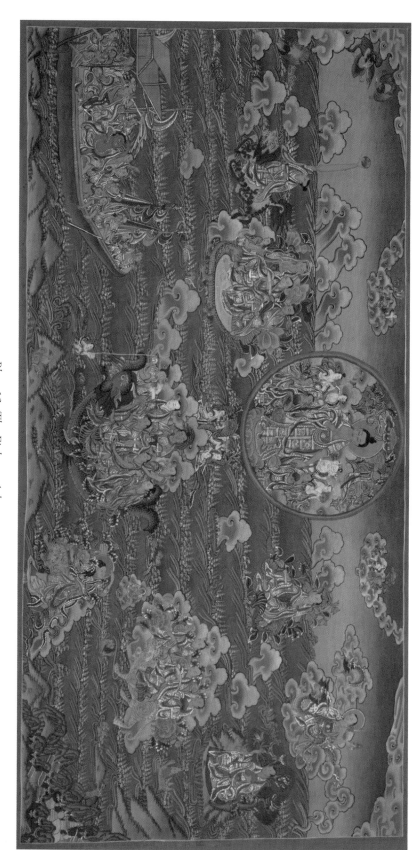

Plate 13. The Eighteen Arhats

from Chinese formal conventions and iconography. The way the arhats have been portrayed is not bizarre, as is often the case in China when people from India are rendered. Then, they often look like caricatures, although this may also have something to do with attempts to portray the arhats' supernatural abilities.

The Chinese emperor had sent the invitation to the arhats in India via a messenger who was the lay brother Hvashang (also written as Hva-san). His name in Chinese simply means "monk," but elsewhere is used as a personal name. Hvashang can be seen down to the right as he travels by ship and guides the arhats. He has a plump appearance and always has a smile on his face. His stout build is a typically positive trait. Often he is depicted with a knapsack full of food. He is known for his generosity and is equated with the so-called pot-bellied laughing buddha we know from Chinese restaurants. This happy figure is always surrounded by tubby little children clambering on and around him. He is a thoroughly trustworthy character and therefore extremely popular.

Hvasgang does not enjoy the same veneration as the arhats, but is usually depicted together with them. This also goes for the layman Dharmatala, who, like Hvashang, is unknown in the Indian tradition. He volunteered to serve the sixteen arhats for the duration of their stay in China.

Dharmatala was known for his erudition. Usually, therefore, he is aptly depicted with a basket full of theological writings on his back. Because he wanted to serve and protect the sixteen, he magically created, out of his right knee, a tiger that protected the arhats from wild animals that roamed the hill where they were staying. In his hand he usually holds a fly whisk to fan the arhats and cool them, and a water bottle to quench their thirst as part of the ceremony before and after prayers.

The portrayal of Dharmatala exhibits a striking parallel with the famous monk Xuan Zang. This monk left the T'ang capital Xi'an in 629 and traveled to India by way of the Takla Makan Desert and the Karakoram Range, to remain there until 645. His intention was to visit holy places and collect Buddhist writings. Back in Xi'an, he translated the writings in the Great Wild Goose Pagoda. His translations have survived. Xuan Zang has the same iconography as Dharmatala.

Avalokiteshvara and other Bodhisattvas

The generic name of the most popular bodhisattva is Avalokiteshvara, the "Merciful Lord Who Looks on Humanity Filled with Compassion" (pictured in Plates 14 and 15 on pages 39 and 40). He has many names and appearances. The number of heads he has varies from two to eleven, the number of arms from two to one thousand. In Nepal, 108 forms of Avalokiteshvara occur that are grouped under the name Lokanatha or Lokeshvara ("Lord of the World"). Lokeshvara is more easily pronounced than Avalokiteshvara. The various forms of Lokeshvara are amalgamations of other Buddhist divinities and Hindu deities.

Another common form of Avalokiteshvara is Padmapani. He has two arms and a lotus (*padma*) in his hand (*pani*). The repeated forms of Shadakshari and Sahasrabhuja Lokeshvara depicted in Plates 14 and 15 are discussed below. In China and Japan, Avalokiteshvara appears in female form, as Kuanyin and Kannon, respectively. Kuanyin is often portrayed as a Chinese Madonna and Child. The reason for the female form is that from an Eastern Asian perspective, compassion and sympathy are none too martial characteristics and befit women more than men. Padmapani's pale color and relatively feminine appearance, certainly in comparison with the trained and muscular body of Manjushri, give him a gentle and understanding look. He is an emanation of the dhyani buddha Amitabha, a likeness of whom Padmapani always wears in his hair.

Avalokiteshvara gained popularity thanks to his unlimited sympathy and endless readiness to help. He came to earth as a bodhisattva to relieve humanity's suffering. He promised to remain and delay his buddhahood until the last person had been set on the right path to bodhi. Every bodhisattva possesses the characteristic traits of wisdom (*prajna*) and compassion (*karuna*). Karuna is most strongly evident in Avalokiteshvara.

In order to help people, or divert them from their erring ways, a bodhisattva can take on all manner of guises, from premier to pimp, from

Figure 9. The mantra OM MANI PADME HUM

dead person to Dalai Lama. Avalokiteshvara is the protective deity of Tibet. The Dalai Lama is considered to be an incarnation of Avalokiteshvara. The palace of the Dalai Lama in Lhasa, the Potala, bears the same name as the mountain where Avalokiteshvara resides.

Shadakshari Lokeshvara

In Plate 14, Shadakshari Lokeshvara sits on a pink lotus and his body always has a white color. He is extremely richly dressed, and slung over his left shoulder is an antelope hide that he can use as a mat to sit on. He has four arms. Two arms are folded in front of his chest in a position that resembles anjalimudra, the gesture of respectful greeting. However, buddhas and bodhisattvas never display this greeting. And so, as could be expected, between the palms of his hands he is holding a *cintamani*, a transparent wish stone that will fulfill all nonmaterial wishes. In his upper left hand he is holding a blue lotus, in his upper right a string of prayer beads. The string comprises 108 beads. The number 108 is one of the holiest numbers in Buddhism. It is composed of the powers of the first three numbers, so 1 to the first power times 2 to the second power times 3 to the third power equals 1 x 4 x 27 = 108. Aside from strings of 108 beads, there are also those with 54 or 27 beads, half or one quarter of 108.

Amitabha appears both in his crown as well as high in the sky, in lotus position, and has the red body color associated with him.

In the foreground are symbols of good luck in the form of the Seven Jewels: elephant tusks, rhinoceros horn, coral, a cruciform accessory, king's and queen's earrings, and pearls. The name Shadakshari (Lokeshvara) means Lord of the Six-Syllable Mantra. By "six syllables," the most well-known mantra (magical formula, mystical syllable) of

Tibetan Buddhism is meant, which is specifically attributed to Avalokiteshvara: OM MANI PADME HUM. Every time a believer utters this mantra, he or she counts off one bead on the prayer bead string that Tibetan Buddhists always have with them.

OM, or AUM, is the cosmic sound that marked the beginning of creation; there are numerous other interpretations in addition to this one. In the mantra OM MANI PADME HUM, OM functions as the initial sound, meaning something like "be well" or "bless you." HUM is the concluding sound, a kind of "amen." Which leaves the widely interpretable MANI and PADME.

With *mani*, jewel, the Buddha or Buddhist teachings are meant. *Padme* means "in the lotus", but in this context, lotus (padma) represents the human heart. Just as a lotus opens in the morning with the rising sun, people should open their heart to the Buddha and his dharma.

Sahasrabhuja Lokeshvara

Depicted in Plate 15, page 40, is Sahasrabhuja Lokeshvara. The basic form for this portrayal is the eleven-headed aspect of Avalokiteshvara, named Ekadashamukha. However, this form has an even more elaborate variation, with one thousand arms, instead of Ekadashamukha's customary eight, and is therefore called Sahasrabhuja.

Nothing arises for no reason, and there is a plausible explanation for the eleven heads. By means of his immeasurable compassion and meditative muscle, Avalokiteshvara managed to empty the hells and ensure that there was potential salvation for everyone. Enthused, he reported this to his spiritual father, Amitabha, who told him to take a look behind himself. Almost instantly the underworlds began filling up again with new sinners who had not escaped from samsara. Sinking into despair, Avalokiteshvara wept so pitifully that his head burst. Amitabha attempted to assemble the pieces but did not entirely succeed. He supplemented the pieces to make nine complete faces, each with a gentle expression. Above this he placed the blue demonic head of Vajrapani that functions to ward off evil, and at the very top, for protection, his own head.

Plate14. The Bodhisattva Shadakshari Lokeshvara

Plate 15. The Bodhisattva Sahasrabhuja Lokeshvara

Four of Sahasrabhuja's eight main arms are identical to Shadakshari's, although here the former is shown with a red lotus. His right hands are in varamudra, the gesture of granting favor, and hold the dharmachakra, the wheel of the teachings. His left hands hold a bow and arrow to symbolize keeping dangers and temptations at a distance, and a kalasha, or water jug, containing the nectar of immortality, amrita, which is a symbol of the deathlessness of nirvana. His 992 other arms are placed like an aureole around the bodhisattva. The idea of a thousand arms is comparable to that of the thousand buddhas: the more the mightier. The eye located in the palms of all the hands means that nobody escapes Avalokiteshvara's great compassion.

At the top of the picture sits Amitabha with the White and Green Taras. At the bottom, in the center, lucky charms lie on a lotus petal. In the lower left, sits the Bodhisattva of Wisdom, Manjushri (see Plate 16, page 42), and to the right is the horrifying goddess, Palden Lhamo.

Palden Lhamo is a typical tantric goddess who belongs in the Vajrayana. Actually she is misplaced in the mild-mannered realm of Avalokiteshvara. Since she appears in this thangka, a brief explanation follows.

Tantric Buddhism recognizes eight dharmapalas, guardians of the teachings. One of them is a woman, but one of the most horrifying kind. She is the Buddhist version of the blood-thirsty Hindu goddess, Kali. Lhamo (her Sanskrit name is Shridevi) rides a mule over an ocean of slaughtered opponents' blood, using poisonous snakes for reins, and her flayed husband for a saddlecloth. Her murderousness is only directed against enemies of the faith. This is why it is not strange that she is worshipped.

In Tibet she is seen as the protector of Lhasa, the Dalai Lama, and the Panchen Lama. In the 19th century it was said that Queen Victoria was an incarnation of her and that Lhasa would not be attacked as long as the queen lived. Whether it was a coincidence or not will never be clear, but in 1904, shortly after Queen Victoria's death, the British Younghusband expedition stood in front of the gates of Lhasa and forced acceptance of a British presence in Tibet.

Manjushri

Manjushri ("Of Pleasing Splendor," "Of Charming Beauty") is the Bodhisattva of Wisdom and Knowledge (prajna), pictured in Plate 16.

He is sitting in the middle of the thangka on a red lotus that rises up above the water. In his right hand, a sword. His left hand is in vitarkamudra, the gesture of giving instruction, while a book is lying on the lotus flower beside his left shoulder. Lower left and right, the White and Green Taras; top left and right, Avalokiteshvara as Shadakshari and Padmasambhava. At the top, in the center sits the historical Buddha.

Manjushri is closely associated with the goddess Prajnaparamita, who is not his partner, but the personification of knowledge, symbolized by the book on the lotus. A book is always rendered as a rectangular packet—a pile of sheets that lies between two flat, wooden lids. Before the 12th century, these were made of palm leaf, later, of paper. Manjushri is the Buddhist counterpart of the Hindu god Brahma, who is also depicted with a book (the Vedas).

With his flaming sword, Manjushri ensures that humans will gain knowledge and insight. He cleaves the clouds of ignorance with it, but also uses it in the morning to chase away the demons of the night, and so brings light into the darkness. This darkness has a double meaning, and is thus also spiritual darkness, ignorance.

Somebody or something's right side is the male side, the left side is female. Waving a sword around is a male-related action, whereas wisdom, as was mentioned earlier, is female, and so is placed on the left.

The entire background of the thangka portrays a green valley surrounded by mountains and boulders. Aside from the deities, the only living beings are pairs of deer and birds, Chinese symbols for longevity. The landscape also has meaning. According to legend, Manjushri came to Nepal from China over 2,000 years ago to worship the Adi Buddha. Surrounded by mountains, in the middle of the country, lay a large lake. In the mid-

Plate16. The Bodhisattva Manjushri

dle of the lake bloomed a lotus on which the Adi Buddha, Svayambhu (the "Self-Creating One"), manifested himself as a flame.

The bodhisattva smote the rocks with his sword near Chobar so that the water flowed away and the valley was able to be cultivated. The present-day Kathmandu Valley lies at the location of the former lake, as has been revealed geologically. He moved the lotus with the flame to a hill on the west side. Later, the stupa of Svayambhunath was erected over it. Manjushri is depicted in red, yellow, golden yellow, white, or black, and almost always sits in lotus position. He is eternally young and muscular, and has some twenty variations.

Manjushri is referred to as an emanation of both the dhyani buddha Amitabha, who is also Avalokiteshvara's spiritual father, and of Akshobhya. This dual origin can be traced back to the fierce form of Akshobhya, the dharmapala Yamantaka, who can take on a fiercer guise, namely Vajrabhairava, and then be an extremely frightening guise of Manjushri. An earthly incarnation of Manjushri is the great reformer Tsongkhapa, the founder of the Gelugpa monastic order.

The White Tara

A late development in Mahayana Buddhism is that the Adi Buddha, dhyani buddhas, and bodhisattvas received female partners. Female bodhisattvas, who appear starting in the sixth century, are called taras. *Tara* means "Star," "Savior," or "Leader." The various taras can be recognized by the color of their skin, among other things. The White Tara appears in the thangka in Plate 17 on page 44.

In the seventh century, Tibet made its entrance onto the international political stage. King Songtsen Gampo (617-649) unified Tibet and conquered parts of China and Nepal. He made two important political marriages with princesses from neighboring countries. Both ladies practiced Buddhism, and therefore Buddhism temporarily gained a solid footing in Tibet. They brought a form of civilization to the then-still-barbaric Tibet.

Both princesses brought buddha figures with them to Songtsen Gampo's court. The Chinese princess Wen-che'ng, a niece of the T'ang emperor, had a gilt figure of Shakyamuni Buddha with her. This jobo was installed in the Jo-khang Temple, Lhasa's most important shrine.

The princesses practiced Buddhism by doing good deeds. Their ensuing popularity and the fact that both remained childless—therefore pure—contributed to their later being identified with the White and Green Taras. Songtsen Gampo was said to be an incarnation of Avalokiteshvara.

According to one legend, Avalokiteshvara once spilled two tears to earth out of pure despair over muddleheaded humanity. Each tear formed a lake in which a lotus grew. When the lotuses opened there was a Tara in the center of each. The tear from his left eye produced the dark-colored Green Tara, the one from his right eye the White Tara. A dark skin tone is often indicated by green. The Chinese princess had a light skin tone, the Nepalese Brikuti was much darker.

Sitatara, or the White Tara, is considered to be a manifestation of Avalokiteshvara. White is the color of purity and therefore she symbolizes immaculacy, and, because of her association with Avalokiteshvara, compassion as well. She is popularly worshipped in Nepal and Tibet. She is sitting with both legs folded under her in lotus position.

Her right hand is always in varamudra, the gesture of offering material and spiritual gifts. In her other hand she officially holds a white lotus, but here she is holding a blue one, which is the attribute of the Green Tara. She has seven eyes: the normal ones, one vertical eye on her forehead, and one in the palm of each hand and sole of each foot. Just as with Avalokiteshvara's thousand eyes, these symbolize the capacity to see all those in need in all four corners of the earth. The little red buddha figure in her headdress is somewhat apocryphal, but not illogical. It represents Amitabha.

Plate 17. The White Tara

Plate 18. The Green Tara

At the top, from left to right, sit a four-armed Avalokiteshvara, Shakyamuni Buddha, and Padmasambhava (see Plate 19, page 50).

At the bottom, in the center, is a table with offerings, and in front of it, one that represents the five senses. To the left are two cymbals, one mirror, and a silk sash; to the right, a shell out of which incense rises into the air, and fruits. These represent the senses of hearing, seeing, feeling, smelling, and tasting.

To the left sits Amitayus, a crowned form of the dhyani buddha Amitabha. His jewelry indicates that he is also considered to be a bodhisattva. Amitayus is holding a jar of immortality nectar in his folded hands, a reference to a sojourn in the Sukhavati Heaven over which Amitabha, or Amitayus, presides, and which became a favorite destination for believers.

To the right sits a goddess with three heads and eight arms, Ushnishavijaya, much revered in Nepal. She is seen as an incarnation of Sitatara. Her title is Mother of All Buddhas, in connection with her superior knowledge. This is why she is holding a little buddha figure in one of her hands.

The Green Tara

In Plate 18, page 45, Shyamatara, or the Green Tara, is sitting, her right leg hanging down, on the lotus in the little lake that formed from Avalokiteshvara's tear. Her right hand is in varamudra, the gesture of giving; she is offering believers her help. The thumb and forefinger of her left hand are pressed together, the symbol of wisdom and compassion, while the three raised fingers represent the triratna: the Buddha, the dharma, and the sangha. She is holding two blue lotuses. She has been depicted as a 16-year-old, because that is the age at which people were considered to be the most perfect and the most consummately beautiful.

Shyamatara offers protection from all dangers, in particular, the eight great dangers: lions, snakes, elephants, thieves, fire, water, demons, and prisons (or the government).

Taras are Buddhist forms of mother goddesses. As such, this is a concept borrowed from Hinduism, which was not unusual, for late Mahayana Buddhism allowed itself be influenced by various Hindu elements. Just as Hinduism recognizes eight mother goddesses, Tibetan Buddhism developed eight taras, although a system of 21 taras also exists.

At the upper left sits Avalokiteshvara, in the center, Amitabha, and in the upper right Sitatara, each on a lotus pillow. At the bottom, in the center, is a bowl of offerings.

Three important factors in Mahayana Buddhism that lead to enlightenment are compassion, wisdom, and strength. These are represented by Avalokiteshvara, Manjushri, and Vajrapani, often encountered in thangkas as a threesome. Manjushri has been depicted in the lower left in Plate 18. To the right stands the blue bodhisattva, Vajrapani. In early Buddhism, Vajrapani is the bodhisattva who stands to the left of the Buddha, while Padmapani (Avalokiteshvara) stands to his right. They are the Buddhist counterparts of the Hindu gods Indra and Brahma. Vajrapani derives his name from the vajra, the thunderbolt that he holds in his right hand. He adopted this attribute from Indra. Originally the vajra was a five-pronged weapon and only later did it gain an esoteric meaning. Vajrapani has many guises, but the strength element is part of his character and is always present. His most frequent manifestations are demonic, as in this thangka, but only with the purpose of offering protection from possible dangers.

V / Vajrayana Buddhism

In the first centuries of our era, a pan-Indian movement began to manifest itself—Tantrism, which derives from the word *tantra,* literally meaning "thread," the warp of a woven fabric. Tantrism lies at the basis of all of India's religions. The most well-known form of Tantric Buddhism is called Vajrayana Buddhism. Elaborating on the idea of weaving, it means a doctrine or ritual system in which everything is connected and interlaced with everything else. Tantras are texts that are ritual in nature, containing a large amount of magic and mysticism. Crucial to Tantrism is an all-pervading duality and polarity. The dualistic concept of microcosm and macrocosm is essential, as are the polarities of male-female, or positive-negative.

Inherent to the idea of polarities is the introduction of female bodhisattvas and goddesses into the pantheon. Eliminating duality in a cosmic sense is usually rendered on the earthly level by sexual symbols, or by what are known as yab-yum divinities. The embrace of man (yab) and woman (yum) represents union.

By means of meditation techniques, yoga, ritual actions, spells (dharanis), magical sayings (mantras), hand positions (mudras), and concentration on groups of deities, the believer tries, coached by his teacher or guru, to eliminate duality. One tries to merge opposites or have them complement each other. The ultimate goal is individual union with what is supreme, merging with the Absolute. In principle, these actions will lead to individual buddhahood within a single human lifetime.

Most knowledge is passed on orally. Because the doctrines and techniques are rarely public or written down, and their contents are cryptic, they are often referred to as "esoteric" knowledge.

Basic Principles of Vajrayana Buddhism

Shakyamuni was the shining example and almost the only one that was venerated in Theravada Buddhism. With the advent of Mahayana Buddhism came bodhisattvas and other buddhas in support of the Buddha. Vajrayana Buddhism developed from Mahayana Buddhism. Here, the historical Buddha still plays a part, but he is a much less venerated figure than, for instance, other buddhas, bodhisattvas, historical saints, or magicians. All of these, with their wisdom, compassion, or tantra tricks, guide receptive people down the path (*yana*), as indestructible and pure as a diamond (*vajra*), to salvation.

In Vajrayana Buddhism, the ultimate reality—emptiness, non-dualism—is portrayed by a vajra, a bolt of lightning. A vajra is a ritual object, but originally, in early Hinduism, the vajra was a weapon belonging to Indra, the god of rain, thunder, and lightning. So the vajra is a thunder-dagger or thunder-wedge, which Zeus, or the Germanic Thor, also wielded. However, considering thunder is difficult to visualize, and thunder and lightning form a unit, the vajra acquired the form of a lightning bolt, an infallible, all-cleaving weapon.

The vajra's lightning aspect in Vajrayana Buddhism evolved into another object that possesses great clarity, a diamond. A diamond is capable of cleaving and destroying without being destroyed itself, just like lightning. Because a diamond is so intensely hard and crystal clear, the mental leap to see the vajra as a symbol of the Absolute, or shunyata, is easy to make.

In Vajrayana Buddhism, one meditates and concentrates on a portrait, a realistic or abstract image, or a painting. The believer identifies with the divinity who is symbolically present in the portrait. The essence of the divinity, or the divinity's strength, flows into the believer. Through concentration on and union with the divinity in this image, one will attain the formless and expressionless state of nirvana. Thangkas fulfill an important role here, both in monasteries as well as in homes.

Vajrayana Buddhism provides a bridge between the sensually perceptible world and the higher world of the pure, absolute truth that possesses neither form nor matter.

Theravada Buddhism with its pratyeka buddhas and arhats is said to be more "ego-oriented" than Mahayana Buddhism, with its altruistic bodhisattvas. However, in Vajrayana Buddhism, which derives from Mahayana Buddhism, the believer is working in an extremely self-oriented fashion in order to attain personal union with the All.

Since the practice of Vajrayana Buddhism is prominent in Tibet, it is also referred to as Tibetan Buddhism. The term "Lamaism" is a misnomer and just as inappropriate as, for instance, the term "Muhammadanism." It is not a religion venerating lamas. A lama is somebody versed in the sutras and tantras. However, not every lama is a monk and not every monastic resident possesses the mental capacities to become a lama.

The Demise of Buddhism in India

Buddhism in India was fabulously popular in waves during the first 1,000 years of its existence. It also became a significant export to Southeast and Eastern Asia. Hinduism was not to be bested, however. At the same time that the worship of buddha figures and the development of a pantheon was getting under way in India, the Hindu world of deities also began to develop. In practice, Hinduism, with its many deities and direct personal worship, became embedded in broader sections of the population than the more elite and intellectual Buddhism. Buddhist universities that were affiliated with extremely large monasteries, such as Nalanda and Vikramashila, were famous centers of knowledge. However, ordinary people could gain little from them. It is striking that Indian teachers who went from these monasteries to Tibet, and Tibetans who went to Indian monasteries to study more regarding the essentials of late Tantric Buddhist teachings, were able to get their teachings to take root in Tibet, but hardly at all in India.

Around 1200, Northern India was plagued by invading Moslems. They obliterated just about everything that crossed their path and whatever was heathen in their eyes. Hinduism recovered, but Buddhism, which wasn't that deeply rooted in the people anyway, disappeared entirely after the monasteries and universities were destroyed. Monks who anticipated this desecration or survived it escaped to Ladakh, Nepal, and Tibet.

Padmasambhava

Over one hundred years after the death of Songtsen Gampo, Buddhism had not made much progress in Tibet. The magical, animistic Bön religion was still practiced everywhere. King Trisong Detsen (755-797) tried to breathe new life into Buddhism. He did this primarily for political reasons, because he wanted to rein in the practices and influence of the shaman priests of the native Bön religion and their Bön following.

He invited the great tantric wizard, Padmasambhava, pictured in Plates 19, 20, and 21 on pages 50, 51 and 53, to his court. Padmasambhava traveled to Tibet from his native region, the Swat Valley in northwest Pakistan, by way of Kashmir and Ladakh. He also brought his teachings to Bhutan where he is still much venerated today. The fact that Padmasambhava was a great theoretician and philosopher, and extremely adept at exorcism and the magic arts were reasons enough to invite him. Padmasambhava succeeded in expelling the demons of the Bön religion, curbing them—and this reveals his skill as a politician—by incorporating them into Vajrayana Buddhism as dharmapalas, guardians of Buddhism. The old tactic—if you can't beat the enemy or drive him away, then let him join you by offering him a function in the new system—worked here. Thus Padmasambhava put into practice one of the essential elements of Tantrism, namely that negative powers and attributes should not be destroyed, but remodeled by adaptation into salutary powers.

Padmasambhava is considered to have been at the basis of the Nyingmapa, the "Order of Elders." The suffix "-pa" indicates the monks in the order.

Tibetan monastic life began taking root in the 11th century as a result of the successful Second Coming of Buddhism. After centuries of having existed with relatively little structure, the Nyingma Order was established in 1062. At about the same time, the Kadam Order, based on the teachings of Atisha, arose. In contrast to the Nyingma Order, the strict Kadam Order advocated celibacy and forbid, among other things, luxuries such as stimulants and money. During the same century, both the Sakya and the Kagyu Orders arose, the latter yielding various offshoots, such as the Karmapa (in Sikkim) and the Drukpa (in Bhutan).

In the 14th century, when it was evident that both believers and monks had let the reins of discipline slip too much, the religiously stringent Gelug Order appeared, and assimilated the Kadam Order.

Guru Rinpoche

The conceptualization regarding Padmasambhava is obscured by legends about his magical feats of heroism. The saint probably did exist, although he became a literary figure in whom several persons merged.

His student, Yeshe Tsogyal, wrote his biography, the *Pemakathang*. Just like many other works, including the Tibetan Book of the Dead (Bardo Thödol), this hagiography was hidden away. Padmasambhava and his followers hid *terma*, supposed treasures, so that they would be found in later times by *tertön*, treasure hunters, people with the proper devotion and understanding. These treasures formed the connecting link between the great guru and modern times. From the eleventh to the 14th century, numerous finds were made.

The honorific title by which he is generally known is Guru Rinpoche, "Precious Teacher." The way in which he has been depicted in the thangka in Plate 19, page 50, is the most customary. He is sitting on a lotus that sprang up in a small lake, is wrapped in heavy, expensive robes, and wears a hat with its earflaps up (it is cold in the Himalayas—the earflaps being up may also be interpreted as the guru's receptivity to prayers and entreaties). He has a vajra in his right hand and a kapala (skull cup) with a little jar of amrita in his left hand, and a khatvanga (staff) clamped against his left shoulder. On his forehead the wrinkles of a frown indicate the hidden wrathfulness that comes to light on exorcising and overpowering demonic forces. Often, the tantric master cocks his head a little. The Sun and Moon, symbols that indicate the guru's cosmic omnipotence as well as his perpetual alertness day and night, have been

depicted on his hat.

He is flanked by his consorts, the Indian princess Mandarava, who stands to his right, and Yeshe Tsogyal, who stands to his left, the two favorite and tantrically most gifted of his five wives. In Tibet he had gained disposal of Yeshe Tsogyal, one of the wives of King Trisong Detsen. She became an extremely devoted disciple and was not too shy to become acquainted with bizarre tantric practices.

The skull cup filled with the nectar of immortality is a symbol of transitory nature of matter, signifying that, for the true believer, death is a joy that leads to the ambrosia of immortality, or nirvana, meaning eternal, timeless shunyata.

Originally, the khatvanga was a club. In Vajrayana Buddhism it became a magic staff used in rituals as a symbol of the highest degree of enlightenment and perfection. The khatvanga is also said to be a substitute for the female partner with whom the yogi (the meditator who practices yoga)—in this case Guru Rinpoche—periodically unites. The staff is crowned with a double vajra (symbol of wisdom and compassion), a jar of life elixir, and three skulls: the fresh head of someone recently deceased, the shrunken head of someone long dead, and a bleached skull. The progression in this series of skulls runs parallel to the rise in awareness (and so to continued extinction) and stands for nirmanakaya, sambhogakaya, and dharmakaya. Topping off the khatvanga is a trident. The trident may symbolize the triratna, but in Tantric Buddhism the meaning is that of the three vertical flows or energy channels that are stimulated by yoga and that rise from the lower body to the skull. Below the trident hang iron rings so that the staff can be used as a jingling beggar's staff (khakkhara).

The Mystical Padmasambhava

Padmasambhava is considered by some as equal to the Buddha. He is called the Second Buddha by the Nyingma Order. The Buddha had many exceptional characteristics. The same was ascribed to Padmasambhava. The Buddha's conception and birth were immaculate events. The same occurred

Plate 19. Guru Rinpoche

Plate 20. The Mystical Padmasambhava

with Padmasambhava, as is revealed by his name which means He Who Was Born from a Lotus.

The mysterious nature of his birth is emphasized by the manner in which the saint is portrayed in the thangka in Plate 20, page 51. He appears like a vision, hidden in an aureole containing all the colors of the rainbow. This manner of portrayal should be interpreted as a mandala (see Plates 34-36, pp. 77, 79, 81). The meditator concentrates on the depiction and finally ends up in the center, at the crux. Almost exactly in the center of the presentation is—all but invisible—the guru's right hand in front of his heart, holding the vajra. The symbolism is clear: the believer's centripetal concentration ends up at the heart of the presentation, at the vajra which symbolizes the *upaya*, the method, to attain liberation.

High in the sky Manjushri, Avalokiteshvara, and Vajrapani represent wisdom, compassion, and strength, characteristics that believers meditating on Padmasambhava need, and are to make their own. The true spirit descends on the reading monks in the little monastery on the shore of the lotus lake. In the lower left sits the Green Tara.

The Eight Guises of Padmasambhava

The eight manifestations of Padmasambhava point to the initiations that the great guru himself had to undergo. He meditated and theorized for a long time and practiced tantric rites so that he kept reaching higher levels in his development.

Guru Rinpoche himself occupies the center of the presentation in Plate 21. He is extremely richly attired and has his standard attributes. To his right sits Mandarava in Indian dress, and to his left sits Yeshe Tsogyal in Tibetan dress. All around, the guru appears in eight different guises. His characteristic hat with earflaps is topped by an eagle feather to show his high spiritual flight, or by a peacock feather as in Plate 19 (p. 50). A peacock is said to be immune to poison. The symbolic value of the peacock feather, then, is that whoever wears it will not be disturbed by the venom in the world that expresses itself in many ways, including temptations and negative thoughts. If there are three peacock feathers, as in Plate 19, this indicates victory over the three major failings or major toxins: desire, hatred, and

ignorance (see the Wheel of Life, Plates 27 and 28, pages 65, 67).

At the very top sits the dhyani buddha Amitabha. Just above Padmasambhava's two partners, sits a group of four figures, which is also depicted below in a second series of four manifestations, two seated, and in the corners, two fierce ones standing.

From top to bottom, and left to right, the guises are: Padmasambhava with his consort, Mandarava, as the blue Adi Buddha in yab-yum, and to the right, portrayed absolutely like a buddha, Padmasambhava as the Second Buddha, called Shakyasimha or Shakya Senge, which literally mean Lion of the Shakyas, an epithet for Shakyamuni Buddha.

To the left, below the Adi Buddha, sits Loden Chogse, the Proclaimer of Wisdom, with a skull cup and a damaru (hourglass-shaped drum made of two skulls covered with leather drumheads, which awaken believers from their spiritual sleep). To the right, portrayed sitting down in almost identical manner, is Padma Gyalpo, or Padma Raja, the "Lotus King," who, with his left hand, is holding a mirror that shows one's karma.

Below Mandarava stands Senge Dadog, a fierce form of Padmasambhava as a dharmapala, surrounded by flames. The guru subdued many native deities and brought them into Tantric Buddhism as guardians (pala) of the teachings (dharma). Here, he plays the part of a dharmapala as he tramples enemies of the faith underfoot. At the same level, to the right, stands a second wrathful manifestation, the demon subduer Dorje Drolo, or Dorje Trolo. Dorje Drolo rides a pregnant tigress, symbolizing that strength and knowledge are latent in everybody. In this form Padmasambhava appeared, flying on his tigress, in Bhutan, where he landed in the Tiger's Lair, the little Taksang Monastery that holds fast to a cliff high above the Paro Valley.

In the lower left sits the wise teacher Pemasambha who is giving instruction, and across from him is an eighth guise, Nyima Oser, the guru, as a gently smiling yogi or siddha, who after years of meditation, was able, in a charnel yard, to catch rays of sunlight in his hands.

This group of eight can also be subdivided

Plate 21. The Eight Guises of Padmasambhava

into four: Guru Rinpoche in the center; to the right above him, the Buddha; directly above him, Amitabha; to the left, the Adi Buddha. These are the representatives of the three levels of dharmakaya, sambhogakaya, and nirmanakaya, with the guru, like a bodhisattva, emanating from the dhyani buddha.

Dakinis and Yoginis

Padmasambhava came from the Swat Valley. In the mountainous country in this region, even under present-day Islam, the belief in *peris*, fairies of the peaks who possess magical powers, is still prevalent. It is plausible that these peris influenced Padmasambhava's view of dakinis. A dakini ("She Who Goes through the Air") is a type of sorceress, an intense type. Dakinis are able to transport themselves through the air in a flash. By traveling this way they skirt all obstacles, and in line with this they also help believers avoid hindrances so as to attain enlightenment faster. Just as the Bön religion has a lot in common with Central Asian shamanism, dakinis can also be placed in this realm. Shamans allow their souls to travel far and wide in order to gain knowledge and bring it back.

Dakinis like to spend time at cremation grounds because this is where earthly bonds are cut and, depending on someone's karma, where the opportunity for enlightenment exists. Padmasambhava meditated a lot in charnel yards, and became acquainted with all the demons of darkness, with visions, and occult powers. He was initiated by dakinis who, air and sky wanderers by nature, linked the earthly and the supernatural, and shared their knowledge of the two extremes with the great guru. For this reason they are said to be initiation goddesses because they initiate the meditating yogi, whoever that might be, into the secrets of Tantrism. They have extraordinary powers at their disposal because they have attained siddhi (perfection).

Due both to their mobile nature as well as their fiery character, they are always portrayed in frenzied motion, dancing, or leaping. Because they are frequently in touch with demons, they often look forbidding. However, in their contact with a yogi they can also take on the appearance of a young yogini (a female yogi) who shares her knowledge openly and frankly with the meditator by uniting with the latter in a sexual embrace. Her nakedness symbolizes that secret knowledge is not veiled by anything and is freely accessible.

Sarvabuddha Yogini

For every dhyani buddha there is an affiliated dakini. A sarvabuddha dakini, however, has access to all the buddhas and thus is more powerful. She is surrounded by a flaming aureole. The thangka in Plate 22 shows the yogini aspect of the dakini. She is standing in what is called the lunging stance to the left, *alidha*. Her body is red, the color of intense emotions and sensuality. Her face shows the same grimness as her dakini figure. With her three eyes she can see past, present, and future. Her jewelry is made of human bones. The strips crisscrossing her stomach are an accoutrement that is only seen on wrathful deities. She is holding a cleaver in her right hand and, in her raised left hand, there is a skull cup filled with blood that she is bringing to her lips. On her left shoulder rests a khatvanga that deviates slightly from Padmasambhava's in that it lacks the trident. The three heads are blue, red, and white here, and are supposed to be of a young man, an old man, and a dead man.

The cleaver, which has half a vajra for a handle and a curved iron blade, is actually a butcher's knife. It is also used to cut up corpses that will receive what is called a "sky burial," in which the cut-up flesh is eaten by vultures and other birds. The ritual meaning in Tantrism lies in the extension of this. It signifies cutting earthly ties and thus crossing into the liberated state.

The kapala filled with blood symbolizes a similar breaking of ties with samsara and also the acceptance of this sacrifice by the yogini who thereby gives positive indication that she will work with the yogi.

Enemies of the faith, who impede the breakthrough to understanding, are trampled under her feet. In the foreground lies a five-senses offering, of the fierce-deity variety: the top of a skull filled with brains, eyes, nose, tongue, and ears.

Plate 22. Sarvabuddha Yogini

Plate 23. The Mahasiddha Tilopa

Mahasiddha Tilopa

A *siddha* is a person who possesses *siddhi,* which is another word for nirvana, but also relates to supernatural powers and qualities that are magically acquired in tantric rites. Anybody—monks, nuns, or laypersons—can become a siddha. It was also already acknowledged in Theravada Buddhism that through utmost concentration, people could develop paranormal abilities, but the knowledge acquired was considered dangerous and was not allowed to be utilized as a method to help others. In Tantric Buddhism there was plenty of room for magic, spells, and exorcism.

Siddhas possess extraordinary, transcendental qualities. Some are able to fly or walk on water; others levitate, are able to become invisible, and transport themselves in a flash over great distances. They are not bothered by heat or cold, are able to go almost entirely without food, and are capable of extending their lives. A siddha builds up knowledge step-by-step, often under the guidance of a guru. One who has a lot of siddhi is called a great siddha, a *mahasiddha* or a Great Perfect One. Around the eleventh and twelfth centuries, biographies of 84 of the most typical mahasiddhas were collected. Here, too, the holy number 84 reappears. Many more of such mystics existed.

The mahasiddhas were historical individuals who lived in India between the seventh and eleventh centuries. These included scholars and poets, but also great minds with no schooling at all. Some were of extremely modest origin, but others were from Brahman and noble families. Some were striking because of their bizarre and unconventional behavior. Of some it might be said that they exhibited outright antisocial behavior, and then there were those who in common parlance were called "crazy."

All had freed themselves of their caste and social background, and were examples of people who did not walk either the path of the ascetic or of the monk. In their own way, answering to neither god nor man, nor taboos nor social norms, not celibate, and radicalizing, they devoted themselves to seeking their own form of perfection. Through their confrontational and libertine

behavior they gained popularity among certain sectors of the population. Some developed into great scholars who put their philosophies into books and gathered droves of students around them, like Tilopa and Naropa.

Only a few visited the Himalayan countries. A number of Tibetan sects trace their origins to one of these mystics.

Tilopa (928-1009) was an erudite guru with many students. Once, during a lesson, he, himself, began to doubt, and a feeling of the senselessness of everything stole over him. Like the Buddha, he snuck away one night, removed his monk's habit, and wrapped himself in the robe of an ascetic. He sat down in a charnel yard. The charnel yard is a typical term in Hinduism and Buddhism. "Graveyard," in the literal sense of the word is inaccurate, because graves are hardly ever dug there. "Cremation place" would be appropriate, except "charnel yard" is a bit more correct because the corpses are laid to rest there before being cremated or processed in some other way. After ten years of meditation and practice, Tilopa had mastered all the siddhi.

Tilopa is often portrayed with a gold fish in one of his hands, as in the thangka in Plate 23. According to legend, Naropa once ran into his guru Tilopa while the latter was frying a fish. He reproached his teacher for killing a sentient being. Tilopa said that he had created the fish magically through the force of his siddhi. He brought the fish back to its original state and let it rise heavenward. The symbolism of the fish should be seen in the framework of the ocean in which the fish ends up. A person's cremains are carried by a river to the ocean. Then, in Darwinian fashion, new life arises again from the waters. A fish swims in these waters. The fact that Tilopa is holding the fish in his hand symbolizes the capacity of the guru to guide receptive souls out of the ocean of rebirth to escape samsara.

In his other hand, the mahasiddha is holding the top of a skull filled with blood as a symbol of the occult powers at his disposal and under his control. Another meaning is, as with the skull accessory in his headdress, that the mahasiddha has conquered death, and, therefore, rebirth.

Plate 24. The Mahasiddha Naropa

Mahasiddha Naropa

At the time that Tilopa was meditating and practicing in his charnel yard, he was assisted by Naropa (956-1040), who later followed him to the monastery of Odantapura, of which Tilopa became abbot.

Naropa had been the abbot of the famous monastic university Nalanda, in Bihar, India. In a vision, he became aware of Tilopa. After eight years, Naropa withdrew from Nalanda and went off as a simple yogi in search of Tilopa. When he finally met Tilopa and greeted him as guru, the latter hit him and chased him away. This steeled Naropa. Year after year, Naropa went from house to house, begging for food for Tilopa, although he received nothing but derision for it. After twelve years Naropa came to a house where wedding festivities were taking place. Here he received sumptuous foods. This was the first time Tilopa showed he was glad, and spoke: "From whom did you get all that delicious food, my son?" Naropa melted with happiness because he had been called "my son," and so had been accepted as a student. He went back to the same house three more times. When Tilopa sent him for the fifth time, he felt ashamed. He stole into a house, removed a bowl of food, and offered it to his guru. Out of devotion to his master, he sacrificed all his good karma with this robbery. However, Tilopa was delighted with his student's deed. He initiated him and gave him a few extremely special spiritual exercises. Tilopa and Naropa are considered by the Tibetan Kagyupa to be patriarchs of their order, yet neither was ever in Tibet.

Telling features of a mahasiddha include eccentric or scanty clothing and bare upper body, sometimes a dark skin color (many were of a low caste and were darker in appearance), an expressive face, dynamic gestures and actions, an Indian physiognomy, wildflowers as jewelry, and often a skull worn as a hair ornament.

In the thangka in Plate 24, Naropa is sitting in a remote mountain world. He is wearing a *yogapatta*, a strap used in meditation to prevent one of the legs from falling to the side. He is sitting on a speckled ground cover, which represents an animal hide. Monks sit on braided mats or on a bundle of grass, but tantric yogis and mahasiddhas exhibit deviant and confrontational behavior. They will sit on the skin of a wild animal, like a panther or tiger, as proof of their philosophy that all forms of pleasure are permissible if they serve the religious method. So they are allowed to eat meat and experience carnal gratification.

Naropa is holding a stylized horn that is supposed to be a ram's horn. It used to be customary in many cultures that during times of epidemics or misfortune, the priests would walk around the town or village blowing on rams' horns, and their sonorous tones would chase away the danger. In the hands of Naropa, the ram's horn symbolizes chasing away ignorance, egotism, and materialism, so that when the appearances of the illusory world have vanished, the road will be open to learn the liberating message of Buddhism. Along with this, Naropa is trumpeting the praises of his guru.

During the 15th century, Chinese influences gradually began to crop up in Tibetan art. From the 17th century onward, Chinese composition and landscapes manifested themselves in Tibetan painting. Tibetan painting was always strongly frontally-oriented with the main personage in the center. Alongside traditional composition with its centrally placed main figure, the off-center placement of personages, originating in China, became fashionable, as can be seen in both of the thangkas portraying the mahasiddhas. Moreover, the gaze is no longer directed straight forward. Another Chinese influence can be seen in the landscapes. An idealization of nature, with bright tones and lots of green and blue, and clusters of rocks in the landscape, is typical of stylized landscapes that do not occur in Tibet itself. This Chinese influence was so great and received such aesthetic appreciation that Tibetans, in fact, never painted Tibetan landscapes.

Milarepa

Naropa's most well-known student was the Tibetan, Marpa (1012-1097), who studied with him in India for sixteen years. Marpa translated various Tantric works into Tibetan, particularly those about yoga. He went to India several times after this for further training. Marpa is seen as the third patriarch of the Kagyupa. He had a large fol-

Plate 25. Milarepa

lowing of students of whom Milarepa, seen as the fourth church father of the Kagyupa, is the best known.

Milarepa (1040-1123) is a historical individual. He wrote the Gurbum, the "Hundred Thousand Songs" (actually, 100,000 words), a book that has been handed down and from which all Tibetans know some poems. As an ascetic he withdrew into caves where he spent years in solitary meditation. Plates 25 and 26 (pp. 60, 62) show him sitting in a characteristic position with his right hand behind his ear, listening to the sounds of silence. Nature was the teacher of his arts, and the inexhaustible source of inspiration for his verses.

Although the various Tibetan monastic orders didn't always get along peaceably, Milarepa is respected by all Tibetans. Shortly after Milarepa's death a student wrote his biography.

Milarepa was born in a well-to-do family. His father died young. He, his younger sister, and mother came under the care of a greedy uncle and aunt who appropriated all their money and land for themselves and shamefully neglected the threesome. On his mother's advice, Milarepa trained himself in black magic in order to exterminate the bad family members. He learned the magic of death and destruction. After his revenge came repentance and remorse. Milarepa ended up finding the great guru Marpa, a scholar with many students. Milarepa moved in with Marpa and his wife. Marpa always retained his married status. Marpa tried him out and put him to the test many times, until finally, true instruction followed. Marpa ordered him to find a cave and to withdraw from the world. The cave was then walled shut with stones, except for a small opening for food. After a long time Milarepa stepped into the daylight again, and reported to his master the knowledge he had gained. Ever since childhood, Milarepa had been known for his good singing voice. He told and sang about the causes and consequences of being born, as represented in the Wheel of Life (see Plates 27 and 28, pages 65, 67).

Milarepa returned to his cave, while Marpa went to India for additional training. Naropa taught Marpa new insights and foretold that on his return to Tibet, Marpa's only son would die, but that Marpa's family line would continue on an intellectual level through his student, Milarepa.

Marpa's instruction to his student included the technique for generating one's own body heat. Those who are capable of this bear the title *Repa*, or "Clad in Cotton," which, in an inhospitable climate like Tibet's, is not the most obvious way to go about warding off the cold!

Milarepa walled himself in again. At a certain point, homesickness made him leave his cave. He wanted to ask Marpa's permission to leave and see his parental home. When he arrived at Marpa's home, Marpa was sleeping. The moment that the first rays of the sun encircled Marpa's head, Marpa awoke, at which moment his wife came in with breakfast. After Milarepa had made his request, Marpa granted him permission, and explained several omens, saying that the fact that he had been asleep when Milarepa came in meant that when Milarepa returned to the hermit's life, Marpa would no longer be alive. The sunlight signified that Milarepa would be the shining light of the Buddhist world and breakfast symbolized that he would survive on spiritual food. When they parted, Marpa told him his last secret knowledge, and revealed to Milarepa the mantra that is handed down only from guru to student, the very mantra that was given by Tilopa to Naropa, who had, in turn, whispered it into Marpa's ear. Girded with knowledge and knowing that all that is physical will eventually come to an end, they consumed a festive farewell meal. During the meal, Marpa manifested himself in various divine guises with the intention of showing the relative and illusory nature of everything. As final advice, Marpa told him not to stray from his knowledge and faith, lest he receive an influx of negative karma, and to withdraw into the wilds of nature, instead of disseminating his knowledge to the bulk of the people because they were too materially-oriented. Finally, Marpa gave him a handwritten scroll that Milarepa was to open only if he found himself in life-threatening danger.

Milarepa found his parental home in ruins, with the skeleton of his mother, who had died eight years before, in it. Therefore, he took up his

Plate 26. Milarepa

life as a hermit again and kept on learning. The rations he had taken along, which were scarce to begin with, ran out after three years. Very close to his cave he found a spring around which thistles and stinging nettles grew. Enthused, he left his hermit's cell, and henceforth meditated at the spring, living exclusively on nettle soup. His body became skin and bones and the hair on his head and his skin acquired a green tinge from his plant diet. His clothes became threadbare. Years passed. His only companionship was the scroll, which, out of respect for Marpa, he sometimes placed on his head.

Once, hunters looking for food passed by. They shook Milarepa up and knocked the emaciated bag of bones that he was rattling to the ground. A year later, another party of hunters passed by. They left a large hunk of meat for him and asked him to pray for the animals they had killed, as well as for them, because they had committed a sin by killing. Milarepa ate the meat with relish, and gained so much strength from it that he attained a higher state of consciousness. In Theravada Buddhism, too, monks had to accept all the food that was put in their beggar's bowl. The meat lasted a long time. When it was crawling with maggots, he at first decided to get rid of them, but then had second thoughts. By eating the last piece of meat he would be robbing the maggots of their food. He went back to nettles.

At a certain moment, Milarepa's meditation stagnated. He realized that that was the greatest danger threatening him because it jeopardized his chances for ultimate understanding. This is why he opened the scroll, and discovered Marpa's instructions in it, including the advice to consume civilized food. At this, his knowledge culminated. He was able to perform miracles, take on other forms, and fly, and had gained telepathic abilities.

Passers-by and visitors were cheered by his instructive songs. He met his sister, who had never wanted anything to do with religion, and he had a positive influence on her. She gave him a blanket which he cut into pieces in order to cover himself as economically as possible. He collected numerous students around him. However, his success also made him enemies. One attempted to poison him. The first time it didn't work, but the second time Milarepa consciously ate the poisoned food. He felt he had reached the end of his earthly existence. Students and others gathered around him to hear his last words. He sang once more and fell into a comatose trance from which he never awoke. Immediately after his death a quarrel arose regarding the dead body and the relics that might be had. Finally, he was peaceably cremated. No traces of ash or bone remained. Milarepa's best relic was his instruction.

His last meal, farewell, death, and cremation strongly resemble the same moments in the life of the Buddha. He, too, died of spoiled food, gathered his students once more, and was the object of greed after his cremation.

The scenery in both of the thangkas picturing Milarepa is a desolate mountain landscape. In both cases, Milarepa has been rendered twice. To the right he sits on his animal skin and meditates, his few possessions nearby. In the background is his cave, with the spring in the foreground. The pot containing the nettle soup is on the fire, and the light-green ascetic is holding a bowl of soup in one hand. In Plate 25 (page 60), Marpa's scroll is hanging behind him. To the left sits the same Milarepa, but now in enlightened state. In the upper left Marpa is sitting on a cloud in the sky, in *padmasana* (lotus position), with both hands hanging down over his knees. He is never dressed entirely like a monk because he never gave up his conjugal life. Garlands decorate the trees, and near Milarepa lie offerings in the form of the Seven Jewels. These objects, taken from Chinese art, may change slightly in makeup. Seen here are mounds of jewels, elephant tusks, coral, round earrings for a king, and square ones for a queen. In Plate 26, in the water, we can see a rhinoceros horn and three jewels with a little crown of flames that represents the triratna.

Milarepa began his spiritual development with black magic. Afterward, he became an ascetic who meditated with the purpose of gaining supreme understanding that way. This is symbolic of the development of Vajrayana Buddhism in Tibet. The Bön religion held sway in Tibet, until Padmasambhava pushed it aside after selecting its useful elements, and the tantras formulated by the mahasiddhas provided the foundation for the monastic orders that further substantiated the tantras and worked them out.

The Wheel of Life

The belief in reincarnation means that shortly after death, the spirit of a person returns to earth in another body or function. The new kind of life in which people end up after rebirth is determined by the manner in which the previous life was lived, or karma, the sum of all acts, reactions, and mental activity. This can come out positively or negatively at rebirth. It may become an oppressive experience, but may also lead to a pleasant or superior life. The thing is, ultimately, to live so purely that one becomes enlightened and attains the state of nirvana. Then one won't be incarnated anymore.

The path to liberation passes by way of three major forms of knowledge: knowledge of one's former lives; knowledge of the lives and deaths of all other beings; and knowledge of how to become liberated from the whole process of samsara. This knowledge can be found in the Twelve-Part Causality Series, the one of cause and effect, as can be seen in the medallions (Plate 28, page 67) and segments (Plate 27, opposite) of the Bhavachakra. *Bhavachakra* means "Wheel of Life," "Wheel of Existence," and symbolizes samsara in the form of a spinning wheel.

People who follow the path of the tantras can attain nirvana, shunyata, in a single human life span, less skilled people will take seven lifetimes to do it, and the slowest people will be born sixteen times before the liberating curtain finally parts. The revelation no longer takes place on Earth, but in heavenly paradises. And if it does take place on Earth, then this will be a repetition and collection of revelations that were already experienced elsewhere in higher realms. Hopeful prospects for the lay community are the Heavens of Amitabha, Maitreya, or Akshobhya. These are pleasant places to bivouac before having to go back to Earth and materialize in a mortal body. Amitabha's Sukhavati Heaven, the Western Paradise, is especially popular. Those who are more developed look farther, and aim for total extinction.

The bhavachakra is an edifying story. This combination of karma, samsara, and nirvana is often painted in the entrances of monasteries. It is intended for simple believers who have no theoretical foundation, but who do know or recognize the stories. In this sense, a portrayal of the wheel of life, with its pictures, is a pauper's bible, as it were, and comparable in intent to the finely worked entrances of medieval cathedrals.

In the center of the wheel, three animals can be seen. They visually represent the three major sins, the most important toxins that are the cause of samsara. The animals are a red rooster, a green snake, and a black pig. They represent desire, hatred or venom, and stubborn ignorance, respectively. The circle around this has a dark half and a light one. In the former, those with bad karmas descend to one of the three underworlds, in the light segment, those with good karmas climb toward one of the three positive heavens. As it happens, people can be reborn into six worlds.

The underworld comprises the kingdom of the animals, where one is subjected to beating and the chance of being eaten (Plate 27, lower left; Plate 28, lower right).

In the kingdom of hungry spirits, hunger and thirst prevail nonstop because the inhabitants have minuscule mouths and an esophagus that is as thin as a needle (Plate 27, lower right; Plate 28, lower left). Their bloating bellies indicate oedema caused by starvation.

The god Yama rules in hell (Plate 27, bottom, center). He has scales to weigh out the deeds of the deceased. Deeds are usually shown as little balls. Bad deeds have dark colors, good ones are white. To the left are those who have been weighed and found too light, to the right are those who have a chance for a better rebirth. The mirror Yama is holding mercilessly shows people the truth. The fires of hell are burning, and people are being tormented by devils.

After death, the spirit, which is eternal, leaves the temporary husk of the body, and enters what is known as Bardo, an intermediary world between death and birth. Here, the spirit has all kinds of visions, both pleasant and terrifying, which can be handled or not, depending on how

Plate 27. The Wheel of Life

one lived during one's earthly existence and how adept one was in religious knowledge and techniques. Lamas and others who were well-advanced on the path to ultimate emptiness are capable of figuring out for themselves where and how they will be reborn.

The positive worlds are those of the demigods and giants who are forever in conflict with their neighbors (Plate 27, upper left; Plate 28, upper right).

The world of humans (top, center) is a good point of departure for attaining nirvana because the human possesses intellect.

In the world of the gods, a carefree life prevails, there are no illnesses, and everything is rosy. The Buddha did not reject the Hindu gods, but made them as subject to karma and samsara as humans, who are the focus of his teachings. In the world of the gods, nothing lasts either, and if their portion of merit is used up, the divinity has to leave and be reborn. Normally, deities exhibit a glow that doesn't fade, they don't feel discomfort, they wear chains of flowers that never wilt, and clothing that always smells fresh, and they don't sweat. If these five aspects begin to change, the deity knows that the time of reincarnation is approaching.

Often, the painter will depict in the six worlds six manifestations of Avalokiteshvara, the ideal bodhisattva for these regions, due to his unlimited compassion.

The outside rim of the wheel are the twelve *nidanas*, the links in the cycle of rebirth. Siddhartha experienced and survived them three times during the night he attained enlightenment.

In twelve medallions, or segments, the nidanas have been depicted, clockwise from the top down and climbing up on the left. In many cases the order is inconsistent and the portrayal will not always be unequivocal. Also, the exact meaning is not clear. The nidanas and their explanations are:

1) Blind old man. Somebody who can't find his way (ignorance);

2) Potter. Shaping matter (karma is formed by transfer; the pots are deeds);

3) Monkey in a tree, leaping monkey. Leaping

here and there (uncontrolled consciousness);

4) Two people in a boat. Name and form, spirit and body (separation between the conscious and the subconscious mind);

5) House with five windows and one door. The five senses (perception); the sixth sense is the capacity to think;

6) Loving couple. Contact arises through the senses (contact);

7) Arrow in eye. Feeling (distinction between pleasant and unpleasant);

8) Woman handing man drink. Wanting, longing ("thirsting for");

9) Picking fruit. Wanting leads to deeds; this nidana is often shown as sex (attempt, act, clutch at, mentally grasp);

10) Bride or pregnant woman; couple in bed. Creation (becoming, coming into being);

11) Birth. New life and consciousness (being);

12) Dead person carried away. At this stage there are two possibilities. Rebirth will take place after a stay in one of the six worlds, and the cycle will recommence. Or extinction will have been attained. Here, this is rendered as a buddha and a bodhisattva in higher realms (Plate 28), or as a direct track (Plate 27, rainbow path) to emptiness which, for artistic reasons, has been depicted as a buddha world, the Buddha in a heavenly palace.

The wheel is held by a monster that has fangs and claws. The interpretations are far from unanimous, but the most plausible is that Mahakala has been rendered here. *Mahakala* is the "Great Black One" or "Great Time." *Kala* means time. Time is seen as the destroyer of everything and everyone, and therefore equated with death. On the one hand time is eternal, without beginning or end, always continuing. On the other, this eternity consists of little portions of time that are finite, like human life.

Gathering of Saints

The kind of thangka depicted in Plate 29, page 68, is called a *guruparampara*, a "Line of Teachers." It shows a family tree, as it were, and its function is to indicate a line of descent. The idea is that the presentation should be seen as a refuge for believers. It creates a kind of structure in the

Plate 28. The Wheel of Life

Plate 29. Gathering of Saints

chaotic number of deities and teachers in whom believers take refuge, because they will help believers in the course of their spiritual development. All the portrayed personages have been brought together in and around a tree that sprouts forth from a body of water. Originally, this manner of portrayal stems from the Nyingma Order, and finds a parallel there in the way in which Padmasambhava was born, namely on a lotus that was growing in a lake. The Gelugpa adopted this idea.

The tree stands in the water. The tree is an ancient symbol throughout Asia. This tree has its roots in the life-giving primal waters, and rises up by way of earth into the higher layers of air, its crown extending into the universe. In cosmic thought, the concepts "tree" and "mountain" are interchangeable. The cosmic mountain, Mount Meru, where the gods live, is also located in the cosmic ocean.

Located in the center of the presentation sits a lama who functions as the believer's guru on the spiritual path. Often, Tsongkhapa is depicted as guide and model. The central figure bears a small buddha figure on his chest which, in turn, also bears a depiction of the Adi Buddha on his chest. This represents the spiritual ascension of nirmanakaya by way of sambhogakaya to the shunyata realm of dharmakaya.

From the central figure, two rays of light emanate and end in congregations of venerable masters who generally represent the Madhyamika and the Yogacara Schools.

The arrangement that is commonly followed in this type of thangka is that the four lokapalas, the guardians of the cardinal directions, are rendered in the bottom row of the tree; above them, dharmapalas and dakinis; next, a row containing the 35 Confessional Buddhas; above them, the important group of deities from the four tantra categories, who point the way to liberation. Yidams, personal guardian deities that are associated with specific tantras, such as Yamantaka, Guhyasamaja, Chakrasamvara, and Hevajra, are often depicted below the central figure's throne.

There are differing grades of tantras. The deities, too, are divided into various ranks. It depends on the level of progress the believer has attained as to which tantra class and deity level should be approached. Study of the tantras is exclusively reserved for adepts, and demands endurance and a certain amount of intelligence. For the bulk of the population it is magic that is dealt with superstitiously.

To the right, above the lama, a series of bodhisattvas and tulkus (enlightened incarnations of religious predecessors) extends up into the sky where, to the right, Shakyamuni sits. In the upper left, in Tushita Heaven, sits Maitreya, the Buddha of the Future, who will come to earth 5,000 years after the Buddha, when the teachings will have dwindled to nothing, and hunger, illnesses, murder, and mayhem prevail everywhere.

The cosmic dimension is also revealed by the presence of the god Indra, in the lower left. Indra, who is riding his elephant, is the king of the Heaven of the 33 Gods who live on Mount Meru. In the lower right, a monk has been depicted to represent the relationship of the believer to the arboreal congregation. The monk is bringing a symbolic offering of the universe in the form of a mandala (see Plates 34-36; pages 79, 81, 83).

The presentation is not only a collection of deities and saints, but is also a concentration aid for the believer who can approach the presentation as a mandala, and penetrate to the essence of veneration by way of the various groups of deities and teachers. This type of thangka is often used to give religious instruction to laypersons and those who are uneducated, and has the same didactic function as the bhavachakra.

This particular tree portrayal often renders a religious tradition that starts off with the founder of a monastic order, for instance, an abbot or a guru. Because believers take refuge in those who are portrayed on the branches of the tree, with their teacher or church father as the central figure, a portrayal of this kind is also sometimes called a Tree of Refuge.

Gurus are expected to follow an unbroken line that goes back to Shakyamuni. So each guru transmits the dharma after having received the teachings and an explanation of them from the guru's own guru. This can be portrayed as many

Plate 30. Tsongkhapa

offshoots on a branch, and many branches on a trunk, while the trunk finally goes back to the roots of the teachings.

Monastic orders often borrowed saints from other orders to include in their own theological tree so that theirs would be more stylish.

Tsongkhapa

Tsongkhapa (1357-1419), pictured in the thangka in Plate 30, was the founder of the Gelug Order. His honorific title is Je Rinpoche. *Je* means exalted. Tsongkhapa was born of poor parents in Amdo, Eastern Tibet, in the Onion Valley. His keen intelligence was evident when he was little. At a young age, he received various degrees from his studies in Central Tibet where he mastered the five main subjects taught by a Tibetan monastic university: *abhidharma* (metaphysics), *madhyamika* (the Middle Way, between Being and Non-Being), *prajnaparamita* (knowledge), *pramana* (logic), and *vinaya* (monastic rules).

The vinaya received his special attention. He abhorred the erosion and the weakening of morals. Because Tsongkhapa had a very sound theological foundation, and was always among the winners in debates, he held a lot of influence. His revulsion toward the laxity in many monastic orders gave rise to the foundation of the Order of the Virtuous, the Gelugpa. Because the Gelugpa lamas wear yellow hats, this order is also sometimes called the Yellow Hats, to distinguish it from the other orders that are called Red Hats. Tsongkhapa restored strict monastic discipline, with the interdiction of the use of alcohol, requirement of strict celibacy, and a tight daily schedule. He attempted to restrict black magic and to resist the erosion of tantric ritual. Still, the Yellow Hats had to make concessions over the course of time, and in performing magical rites had to call on the Red Hats and Black Hat Sorcerers. Tsongkhapa founded large monasteries and universities, such as Ganden, Drepung, and Sera.

Almost 400 years earlier, Atisha, the founder of the Kadam Order, had also tried to clean house at one time, so the Kadampa was readily absorbed into the new Gelugpa.

Due to celibacy, the possibility of hereditary successors vanished. This made way for a line of reincarnation. Someone who is to be designated as a new monastery abbot or lama is considered to be an incarnation of his predecessor. Out of this grew the succession of Yellow Hats leadership, the Dalai Lama, who is an incarnation of Avalokiteshvara. The line of Dalai Lamas began in the 16th century. After his death, Tsongkhapa retroactively became the first Dalai Lama. The Dalai Lamas gradually acquired secular rule over Tibet as well, because the Gelug Order grew, although not without a struggle, to become the most important monastic order in Tibet. The fifth Dalai Lama, who transferred the administrational seat to Lhasa, and who began building the Potala, selected the lama of the Tashilunpo Monastery as an incarnation of Amitabha and conferred on him the title of Panchen Lama. The Panchen Lama was henceforth considered to be the supreme spiritual authority in the country. From a purely religious perspective, the Panchen Lama hierarchically ranks higher than the Dalai Lama because Amitabha is the spiritual father of Avalokiteshvara.

Analogous to Shakyamuni and Padmasambhava, a whole series of legends grew up around Tsongkhapa, and he gained his own iconography. The major moments of his life and his eight most important students were often portrayed. This is the case in this thangka, but the painter did not do much research to render the typifying details. Another curious thing is that Tsongkhapa is not wearing his characteristic yellow hat. What is correct are the two standard attributes he always has, namely a sword and a book that are lying on a lotus at the height of his shoulders. Due to his enormous wisdom, Tsongkhapa was compared to the Bodhisattva of Knowledge, Manjushri. This is why he has the same attributes. Still, in the upper left we encounter Avalokiteshvara in his eleven-headed form. The logic of this is that the Dalai

Lama's incarnations are of Avalokiteshvara, and Tsongkhapa is the first in the line of reincarnation of the Gelugpa abbots. Usually he holds his hands in dharmachakramudra. The way he has been rendered here, although not unusual, occurs much less often: with a little jar of amrita in his left hand. Considering amrita stands for nirvana, this then concerns the ambrosia of deathlessness. The meaning of this is that Tsongkhapa is the great guide on the way to liberation.

Yidams and Dharmapalas

There are two main groups of terrifying deities: yidams and dharmapalas. A dharmapala is a guardian of the teachings. A yidam is a personal guardian deity. Believers choose one during their education or have a deity designated by their guru. At the end of his or her education, a student receives a secret mantra from his or her teacher that belongs to the chosen deity and through which the student can come into contact with that deity. This mantra is the student's secret alone.

Yidams are also personifications of tantra systems, such as of the Kalachakra Tantra or the Hevajra Tantra.

On the path to buddhahood, for which all believers attempt to strive in principle, believers will meet all kinds of stumbling blocks and pitfalls. These are their own forms of ignorance and weaknesses, and need to be overcome. The yidam is helpful in this. Depending on the character of the believer, the yidam may be peaceful or fierce. Friendly yidams are usually buddhas, in yab-yum or not.

A fierce yidam is nothing but one's own pent-up, intense ferocity that needs to be seen as a positive explosion of energy. It is not a rage directed at someone else, but precisely at one's self, namely against the annoying undercurrents in the mind that stand in the way of a breakthrough to total understanding. These undercurrents need to be cleared up because they are forms of ignorance. They are visualized as people that are trampled underfoot.

A yidam is an archetype, a divinity that represents an unconscious idea and an primeval image from the collective consciousness. Through concentration and meditation, an image like this can be called up from the most profound depths of the subconscious.

A yidam is at the same time a portrayal of the practicing, believing self, according to the notion that the divinity is called up in one's own heart. Considering the yidam is, after all, one and the same as the believer, meditators can also first direct their concentration to the yidam so that it will descend into their mind to protect, coach, and advise. Whenever one is bothered by one's own obstructing undercurrents, or, for that matter, surface currents, such as clinging to the pleasure-seeking life too much, complaining too much about both large and small adversities, or showing too little force of action and character, then the wrathful yidam will appear in its murderous and bloodthirsty-looking guise. This seems horrifying and scary, but at the moment that believers banish their ego to the background, the yidam will reveal itself in its peaceful guise.

The glow you can feel in the process of intense thought, rage, or joy, translates into an aureole of flames in the portrayals of yidams.

Kalachakra

Kalachakra, featured in the thangka in Plate 31, is the favorite yidam of the Gelugpa. The Dalai Lama gives frequent Kalachakra initiations.

Kalachakra has four heads, twelve pairs of arms, and one pair of legs. He stands in yab-yum with his partner, Vishvamata, the Mother of All, who is always orange. Kalachakra tramples Hindu deities underfoot. With his right leg, Kamadeva, the god of love, and with his left, Rudra, a form of Shiva. Beside Kamadeva lies his spouse, Rati, and beside Rudra his wife, Parvati.

Below the lotus on which the yidam and his prajna stand, a triangle points downward. This is as the point of a magic dagger, *phurbu*, that is used to nail down dangers and symbolic enemies of the faith. Here, its edges have been trimmed with skulls, and the symbolism is clear: conquering death and thereby putting an end to the cycle of rebirth.

At the top, in the center of the flaming aureole that surrounds Kalachakra and his partner, the blue Hevajra dances. Hevajra, who can be recognized by the skull cups in his hands, is the Buddhist version of the Hindu god Shiva, in his guise as Nataraja, King of the Dancers.

Kalachakra means Wheel of Time. It is one of the last great tantras and dates from the 10th century. The mahasiddha Naropa wrote a well-known commentary on it, and the reformer Atisha brought the Kalachakra Tantra from Bengal to Tibet.

In the Kalachakra Tantra, Kalachakra is the name for the Adi Buddha. Wisdom (prajna) and emptiness (shunyata) are identified with time (kala), while the active element of the method (upaya) is brought into the context of the wheel (chakra). The union of kala and chakra brings the bodhi into being.

Meditating believers are capable of visualizing the entire cosmos in themselves and of identifying themselves with the Adi Buddha. Along with the spatial aspect, the element of time (kala) has also been incorporated here.

Chakrasamvara

A yidam who strongly resembles Kalachakra in manner of depiction is Chakrasamvara, shown in the thangka in Plate 32. The Nepalese thangka painters themselves have trouble distinguishing them. Even though they might not follow the iconography entirely, one can still tell from a few characteristic traits whether or not the yidam is Chakrasamvara. This yidam is usually shown holding the head of the Hindu god Brahma in one of his hands. Brahma can be recognized simply by his four faces. Chakrasamvara has a staff in one of his upper hands and a flaming jewel in his hair.

Chakrasamvara is an emanation of Akshobhya, as is Hevajra. He is also sometimes called a form of Hevajra.

Beside the blue gate with its typically round, Chinese form, in the red wall on the left, halfway to the edging of the thangka with its Chinese dragons, the three figures of Mongolian horseback riders at the bottom of the picture are striking. The central one, holding a banner in his right hand, is the guardian of the cardinal direction north, Vaishravana, who rides a snow leopard. Vaishravana is the Buddhist version of Kubera, likewise associated with the north, the Hindu god of wealth whose Buddhist counterpart is Jambhala (see Plate 37, page 87).

The guardians of the cardinal directions, or lokapalas, guard against dangers that may come from the four cardinal directions. These Four Great Kings are almost always painted in the front entrances of monasteries, the place where the bhavachakra will also be depicted. The lokapalas flanking Vaishravana have not been rendered here with their typical iconographic traits, so that it is hard to say who is Dhritarashtra, the Lord of the East, or Virudhaka, the Guardian of the South, or Virupaksha, Lord of the West. Only on the basis of the colors of their bodies can a suggestion be given. Vaishravana, Lord of the Yakshas, is yellow. The rosy red one could be Virupaksha, Lord of the Nagas. Dhritarashtra, Lord of the Heavenly Musicians (gandharvas), is white. In which case, Virudhaka, the blue-green Lord of Giants (kumbhandas), is missing.

Herukas

What is striking about Vajrayana Buddhism are the numerous demonic figures with their multiple heads, various limbs, and their bloodthirsty expressions brimming with murderous intent, that are sometimes standing or dancing in intense sexual fusion. The yab-yum portrayal is, technically viewed, a sexual position, but actually concerns a non-orgasmic action that is meant to express the elimination of duality.

In a ritual sense, duality is also eliminated by two of the most important attributes that believers can hold in their hands and that a divinity will also often hold. They are the vajra and the ghanta. The vajra represents the male aspect and the ghanta the female aspect, as well as method and knowledge respectively. In order to attain understanding, knowledge (prajna) is necessary and, armed with knowledge, the proper method (upaya) is needed to allow this knowledge to operate so that benefit can be derived from it. In Tantric Buddhism the pairing of these two is portrayed by bringing vajra and ghanta together, as

Plate 31. Kalachakra

Plate 32. Chakrasamvara

Figure 10. Vajra and ghanta

can be seen in the hands of the major, male divinity. This is a symbol for eliminating duality in the same way as the yab-yum portrayal.

In general terms, it is often said that these savage types protect Buddhism from enemies that threaten the faith in all manner of guises and from all directions. In their function as yidam, they protect the individual believer. Many will have a special place in the monastery close to the holiest part of the complex or near the main altar. Others will reside in a separate temple space, the *gonkhang*, and guard the entire monastery complex from there.

Herukas are yidam deities that are portrayed in yab-yum with their prajna, as in the thangka in Plate 33. As wrathful deities, accessories and attributes have been adapted to their character. Their headdresses consists of five small death's-heads, the fierce variant of the crown of five flower petals that would indicate the five dhyani buddhas, had this regarded a peaceful divinity. The long necklace is formed by skulls strung together. In their hands, a drum made of the tops of two skulls, a skull for a drinking goblet, a staff, and intestines. The most frontal pair of hands holds the vajra and the ghanta against each other.

The five dhyani buddhas each stand at the head of what is called a buddha family, a gathering of buddhas, bodhisattvas, and other divinities, that is grouped under one umbrella term. The dhyani buddha Akshobhya has a vajra as his characteristic trait. The buddha family over which he presides is called the vajra family. The terrifying manifestation of Akshobhya is called Vajra Heruka. Herukas are thus the fierce forms of the dhyani buddhas. Heruka is both the name of one particular divinity as well as the label for a type, a heruka. With the earlier opinion that believers identify with their yidam in mind, a heruka is a fierce, deified form of the yogi himself.

The yidams of the old, non-reformed Red Cap sects will often have wings. Also from the partially exorcist ambience surrounding these early Red Caps, come the deities with animal heads who serve as a lower order of guardians. These same figures will appear to the deceased in Bardo as visions. Red Cap lamas and the Adi Buddha, Vajrasattva, with the vajra on his chest and the ghanta at his left hip, sit at the top of the picture. In this thangka the herukas are grouped like dhyani buddhas.

A well-known heruka is Hevajra who is the yidam of the tantra system of the same name. This fierce emanation of Akshobhya is the deified formula "O Vajra," or "He Vajra."

Mandalas

In all cultures, humans have tried to order their relationships with the cosmos and to systematize nature and the natural phenomena around them. Relationships with the cosmos can be most clearly seen in a mandala. *Mandala* literally means "magic circle" or "ring," but in practice it is a geometric pattern of squares and concentric circles as a projection of the cosmos. Three splendid examples are shown in Plates 34, 35, and 36 (pages 79, 81, and 83).

A temple floor plan can be seen as a duplicate of this projection. This concretization of an idea is strongly developed in the stupa. A stupa is an architectonic, three-dimensional rendering of the universe. By means of spiraling and, if possible, getting closer and closer to the center, the believer will arrive at the essence. The most beautifully

Plate 33. Herukas

built example is the late 8th-century stupa of Borobudur on the Indonesian island of Java. The believer walks through galleries that become smaller the higher one goes. Literally and figuratively one rises, in altitude and in understanding, and gradually gets to the core of the matter that, in this case, is a stupa on the top. The stupa is the symbol of death, namely of conquering death, thus of escaping samsara. On a two-dimensional mandala the same thing happens, although one takes a visual, rather than physical, walk to the core of understanding. From the outside of the presentation the believer moves by way of the depicted groups of deities toward the center of the mandala where the major deity or a symbol is the ultimate goal.

Like the stupa, a mandala is a psychogram. Originally the mandala was a cosmogram. However, due to the strong resemblance between macrocosm and microcosm, the mandala also represents the disintegration and then reintegration of one's own consciousness.

A mandala can be drawn or made on the ground with meticulously sifted colored sand. After the conclusion of the rite the mandala is removed. Over the course of time the mandala lost its original function as temporary aid at initiation rites, and merged with the thangka. Thus the painted mandala became an everyday object of veneration, but without its function as specific meditation object or liturgical aid.

In their meditation and devotion, in order to reach emptiness, believers make use of the opposite of emptiness, namely, symbols and presentations of deities with their attributes. By means of deep concentration on emptiness and uttering a dharani (saying) or a bija, a magical syllable that indicates very concisely a deity's pith or essence, the deity is summoned. This deity will be an aid in their meditation.

Another aid is a large, organized group of deities, a group of symbols, or—on a more abstract level—only bijas, brought together in one mandala.

Believers can also identify with the goal by way of yoga. Instead of making use of an aid that has physical form, like a thangka or an image of a deity, one can take one's own body as the point of departure to attain unity with the divine. By means of concentrated energy rising up along the spine, one attains the apotheosis of the process of union in a lotus-shaped mandala at the crown of one's head. This is where light breaks through the spiritual darkness. The thought behind this is that, according to the tantras, humans are vessels full of ignorance, but also vessels with a divine spark in their most profound depths. It is invisible due to the darkness of ignorance, but is the same as the heavenly essence. Yoga means linking, the linking of body and spirit or spirit and cosmos, or microcosm and macrocosm. Still another symbol of this union is combining the vajra and ghanta.

The Mandala of Yama

Yama, depicted in the mandala in Plate 34, is one of the eight dharmapalas. A dharmapala—either male or female (one dharmapala, Palden Lhamo, is a woman)—protects the teachings against attacks from the outside (by demons or enemies of Buddhism) and from the inside (by heretics). Like many other deities in Buddhism, the dharmapalas were adopted from Hinduism. In the specific case of the guardians of the teachings, these were originally enemies. Once converted, the often demonic deities became fiery defendants of their new belief. Yama, the Hindu god of death, appears already in the Rig Veda (ca. 1200 b.c.e.).

The number of dharmapalas was expanded to the sacred number of eight only relatively recently. Before the 16th or 17th century, the octet would be supplemented with several portrayals of one dharmapala. There are also scenes known to comprise eight depictions of Yama.

In Hinduism, Yama is the ruler of the south. While the north is positive and associated with wealth, the south is negative and the region of death. Yama, who rides a water buffalo, governs the south as Lord of the Hereafter.

Plate 34. The Mandala of Yama

Buddhism adopted Yama, albeit that unlike in Hinduism, he was portrayed with a bull's head and received his own iconography. The old tradition of his incestuous relationship with his sister, Yami, was retained.

Yama was once an ascetic who had withdrawn into a cave. One day, two cattle rustlers who had stolen a water buffalo showed up. They entered the cave where they wanted to slaughter the animal. While they were at their task, they noticed the ascetic in the back, meditating in silence. In order not to have any witnesses to their crime, they killed the devout man by beheading him. Yama had meditated and practiced penitence for a lifetime and was only one day away from ultimate understanding. After he was killed, he immediately sprang to life thanks to the enormous amount of positive strengths he had gathered during his life. He placed the head of the water buffalo on his own headless body and killed the twosome. In his frenzy he couldn't stop, and threatened to exterminate everything and everyone in Tibet. In desperation the population called on Manjushri for help. He took on a fierce guise and managed to calm Yama down, as Yamantaka (the "Subduer of Yama"). Both are much venerated.

There is an interesting parallel to this Buddhist legend in Hinduism. There a fierce form of Vishnu rages around with the same disastrous consequences. Shiva is the one who has to calm down the fierce Vishnu.

The rage and the intensity of a dharmapala should be taken as a metaphor for the individual struggle of the believer against all kinds of obstacles. Dharmapalas are also frequently personifications of the collected negative qualities of the deceased. In this case, Yama, as the god of death, is very appropriate in this context.

In this thangka, Yama and his sister Yami can be seen at the four corners as well as within the mandala, all the way to the center. At the bottom are the sacrifices of the five senses, of the fierce-deity variety. The charnel yard spectacles fit in very well here with the symbolism of the destruction and banishment of the ego on the way to liberation. The five-senses offering can be interpreted as offering one's own "I."

The Kalachakra Mandala

A mandala is surrounded by a ring of fire. In the thangka in Plate 35, the fire has been rendered florally in rainbow colors. Fire in Tantrism means knowledge. Without knowledge (prajna) there is no possibility of arriving at supreme understanding. Here, fire also means that believers who enter the mandala are purified, as it were, and at their passage through the purging fire, their ego and all their illusions will burn away.

After this comes a circle of vajras that indicates the transition to the world of knowledge. Thangkas that contain terrifying deities will have a ring containing eight charnel grounds (see Plate 34, page 79), which symbolize the eight feelings and mental activities that bind people to samsara and therefore need to be destroyed.

Then there is a circle of lotus petals (see Plate 34). Here the spiritual realm begins and one enters the mandala.

In the case of this Kalachakra mandala, as shown in Plate 35, instead of the lotuses, eight dharmachakras that refer to the historical Buddha setting the wheel of the teachings into motion, have been painted. Letters between the wheels indicate various deities.

In Asia it is believed that the cosmic mountain, Mount Meru, where the gods live, is in the center of the cosmic ocean.

The Kalachakra mandala has at its center Mount Meru with the four corners of the world around it. On a flat plane, only the projection of this can be seen. The four corners are rendered as four gates that are each colored differently. Each cardinal direction is indicated by a color. The elements of earth, water, fire, air, and ether that are symbolized by the structural portions of a stupa and that are thus also present in Mount Meru, are indicated in the mandala by the various squares. Through the entrance gates, the believer gets inside the mandala. Guardian deities in chariots protect the gates.

The basis of the painted mandala is always formed by two crossed vajras. Only the points of the vajras can be seen. In Plate 36 this is more obvious than in Plate 35, where the ends of the vajras have been worked out into the gate structures.

Plate 35. The Kalachakra Mandala

According to tradition, Shakyamuni Buddha is supposed to have communicated the Kalachakra tantra in the mystical land of Shambhala. In the heart of Shambhala, in the center of a palace with nine stories, is a large Kalachakra mandala.

Shambhala is a mythic kingdom, comparable to the "pure countries" mentioned earlier, and it lies somewhere to the north of Tibet, surrounded by high, snowy mountains. Shambhala is a paradise on earth. Its people are not acquainted with illnesses or hunger and nothing but happiness prevails. This practically unattainable utopia can only be found by people who are sufficiently pure of spirit and free of ignorance. The Panchen Lamas are said to reincarnate as kings of Shambhala.

This enviable paradise led to numerous literary and artistic speculations in the West. The one that became most famous was the creation of the ideal world of Shangri-La in the James Hilton novel *Lost Horizon*, first published in 1933.

The All-powerful Ten Mandala

In Plate 36, in an idyllic landscape—with the White Tara, the dhyani buddha Amitabha, and the Green Tara at the top, and, at the bottom, the trio Manjushri, Avalokiteshvara, and Vajrapani—there is a nonfigurative mandala depicted in the center. The symbol at the heart of this mandala is called the All-powerful Ten. It occupies an important place in the Kalachakra rites.

The All-powerful Ten is a mystical symbol that was written more than a thousand years ago on the wall of a monastery in Nalanda (Bihar, Northeastern India). It is made up of seven letter symbols (ya, ra, va, la, ma, ksa, and ha) and the three symbols for Sun, Moon, and flame. It symbolizes various cosmic systems and the relationship between microcosm and macrocosm. The interpretation is extremely complex and not to be summarized in a single explanation. A closer look at the contents will follow an initial explication, and the same symbols will be explained again, but at a higher lever.

A few meanings in brief. *Ya* is the mandala of the wind, *Ra* of fire, *Va* of water, *La* of Earth, *Ma* is Mount Meru, *Ksa* symbolizes *kamadhatu* and rupadhatu, the realms of wanting and form, *Ha* is *arupadhatu* or the Realm of Formlessness. Sun and Moon symbols correspond with ether, and the flame is the *bindu*, the center of the universe and symbol of total extinction. These ten are associated with different colors. All ten are also related to different body parts and chakras (energy centers) that are accentuated in yoga and yogasanas (positions) and exercises.

The divine nature of the symbol is revealed by the fact that it is placed on a lotus throne. Anyone meditating on the All-powerful Ten will incorporate the entire cosmos through this yantra (object of meditation).

Plate 36. The All-powerful Ten Mandala

VI / Paubhas

The painting in Plate 37, on page 87, is a paubha. *Paubha* is the Newari word for a religious painting on canvas. In paubhas, as a rule, there is a strong emphasis on a centrally portrayed human or divine figure, but mandalas and sacred buildings also appear. The Buddhist Newari will use the paubha as an aid in meditation, hang it above the altar at home, or commission one to be painted because it is a worthy act that will positively influence their karma. On festive occasions they used to display the painting publicly, but this custom has decidedly lapsed.

This paubha involves a Buddhist presentation, but, unlike thangkas, paubhas will also have Hindu themes.

Stylistically, modern paubhas exhibit little difference from thangkas. What distinguishes them is that in paubhas Tantric deities are less intense, the central figure generally sits under an elaborate, ornamental arch that will have a lion mask at the top, or a garuda holding two snakes, and at the bottom, often on a small scale, the commissioners of the work, dancers, and musicians will be painted.

Vasudhara

In Buddhism, Vasudhara is seen as Jambhala's partner. Both are deities associated with prosperity. They are the Buddhist counterparts to the Hindu god of wealth, Kubera, with Vasudhara as a partner, who is also worshipped as Bhumi. Bhumi is an earth goddess who is summoned in connection with the fertility of the land. However, as goddess of happiness and prosperity, Vasudhara is also the Buddhist counterpart to the Hindu goddess Shri, or Lakshmi.

Hinduism as well as Buddhism strives for an immaterial existence and ultimately for detachment, and both attempt to have earthly life pass as pleasantly as possible. For a carefree existence, prosperity as well as a dearth of troubles and obstacles are necessary. This is why deities who can ensure these things are venerated.

This painting is filled with elements in this vein, such as good spirits, deities connected with wealth, and symbols and elements that have to do with prosperity.

The Buddhist Vasudhara is a goddess whose name means "Possessing a Fortune," "Overflowing with Riches."

The whole tenor of the painting is that of prosperity, wealth, and success. She is particularly popular among the Newari of the Kathmandu Valley.

Her skin color is always golden yellow, the color of ripe grain. She will be clothed in a colorfully woven lower garment and adorned with ornaments and jewels. She has three pairs of arms. In her upper right hand she is holding a rosary. In the middle hand a little urn with three jewels in it, while she has her lower right hand in varamudra, the gesture of giving or granting, that is, giving something in the actual, material sense or granting a favor; a lotus has been painted in the palm of her hand. Her left hands are holding the Book of Wisdom, a sheaf of ripe rice, and a metal pot covered with foliage and gemstones.

The grain heads and the jewels connect her directly with the primary occupations of the Newari, namely agriculture and trade.

There is a three-way split in the disposition of her hands. The top two symbolize religiosity and spiritual well-being, holding the rosary with which believers count their prayers and the book in which knowledge and wisdom are written. The middle pair represents the material aspect, what is earthly, possessions. The jewels indicate prosperity, but simultaneously entail a religious component, because they symbolize the Three Jewels of Buddhism (the Buddha, the dharma, and the sangha). The meaning of the rice is a harvest surplus, thus sufficient food, and therefore prosperity. Her two lower hands stand for physical well-being. The goddess gives or grants, so humans receive, while the urn is considered to contain both gemstones as well as amrita, the nectar of immortality.

Just as Jambhala is accompanied by yakshas and yakshis, these male and female earth spirits can be encountered among Vasudhara's retinue. Originally, they were pot-bellied dwarves and gnomes that lived close to the ground in mountains and forests, where they were guardians of the treasures of the earth. The earth provides treasures in the form of vegetation and rich harvests, but also gemstones and minerals that come from mines that are generally found in mountains. The Hindu god Kubera was originally a yaksha, but later became the leader of the yakshas. Jambhala is the Buddhist adaptation of Kubera, the guardian of the cardinal north. The figures below Vasudhara's throne are further developed forms of yakshas and yakshis. Some are slightly corpulent, others look like normal people but have pointy ears, and there are some with animal heads. They carry sacks and baskets that are undoubtedly filled with riches and expensive metal platters piled high with offerings.

Beside Vasudhara's throne, four accompanying goddesses have been depicted, having the same appearance and attributes as the major goddess.

Vasudhara is sitting in mountainous surroundings. Mountains inherently bear a relationship to prosperity. After all, mountains metonymically mean the Himalayas, and thus the cardinal north, associated with prosperity. Moreover, from mountains come rivers that bear primarily fertility-bringing water, but that also wash down precious metals and jewels. In the mountains lie mines that produce gemstones. Various kinds of trees have been rendered on the rock designs. Green trees are connected with growth and fertility. Vasudhara is sitting on a throne in lalitasana. Lalita is a relaxed sitting position (asana) in which her folded left leg rests sideways on the pillow and her right leg is partially pulled up but hanging down. Her right foot is resting on a lotus on which there is a metal urn, the mouth of which is sealed by the shell of a sea snail—that of a white conch—both auspicious symbols of abundance. Jambhala, too, usually has an urn or pot filled with jewels under one of his feet.

The throne consists of an architectonic base where niches in which lions' and elephants' heads, the latter partially hidden behind a red drapery, can be seen. On it lies a lotus with multicolored petals that has a half-moon resembling a white pillow on it, on which the goddess sits. While the Sun is a male heavenly body, the Moon is femi-nine. The Moon is associated with rainwater and the nectar of immortality that fall to Earth as "Moon drops" and ensure fertility, a phenomenon associated with women.

The two-part back of the throne has arched forms and is edged with gemstones. The high-rising sides have been painted analogously to the Bengal thrones of 1,000 years ago, as were known from stone carvings and bronze figures. Usually the bottom is formed by an elephant and on the elephant's back, a rearing lion. In this painting, a kind of local variation on the German fairytale about the street musicians has been portrayed, with a hybrid creature with a floralized tail on top of the lion, and on top of it a green griffin-like creature with a rider. The crown of the throne is formed by a garuda on top, flanked by green nagas, or snakes, and two celestials, while underneath these sit two pink *makaras*, compound water creatures with something of a crocodile jaw and an elephant's trunk, and a body that is engulfed among elaborate floral tendrils.

Jambhala and Ganapati

Two important deities have been depicted in the upper corners. To the right, on a snow leopard, sits Jambhala, with a victory banner in his right hand that indicates Buddhism's victory, and in his left, a nakula, a little rodent that is something between a civet, in looks, and a combative weasel, in character, known in English as a mongoose.

Rudyard Kipling immortalized the nakula in his story "Rikki-Tikki-Tavi" in the fight between the mongoose and its archenemy Nag, the cobra. In the fight, the nakula gains the advantage and kills the naga, the snake.

The Southern Asian attitude with regard to snakes is ambivalent. Snakes are unpopular creatures on the one hand, as the venomous bite of some kinds is dreaded. On the other, a snake that slithers over the earth and that often keeps itself near or in water, is associated with water and so is connected with fertility. Moreover snakes are reputed to be the guardians of treasures. The earth provides riches, such as abundant harvests. However, it also hides mines from which precious stones and metals can be extracted that are guard-

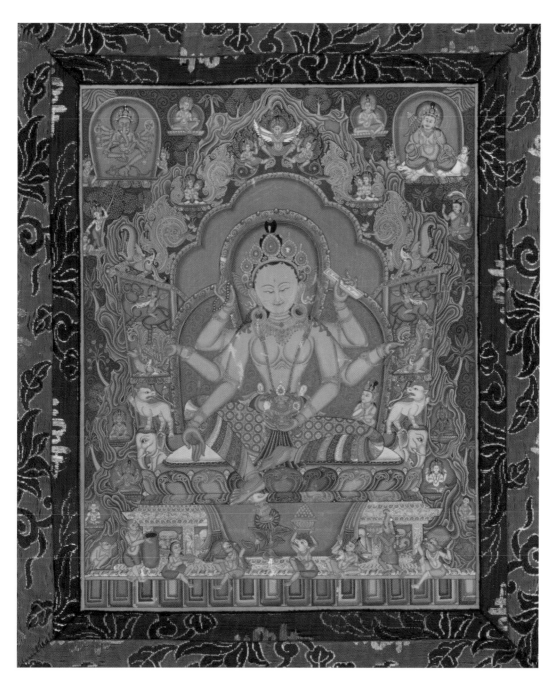

Plate 37. Vasudhara

ed by nagas. If in a legend a snake is killed by a nakula it is clear that the guarded treasures will transfer into other hands. In this case the nakula is swallowing them. This is why it is logical that the nakula would supplement the god of prosperity, Jambhala, and that the little creature is depicted spitting out jewels. In this paubha the stream of jewels is not very visible, but is suggested by the folded hands of the little white figure that catches the stream from the nakula's mouth.

Just like the yakshas, Jambhala is depicted as being corpulent. Corpulence is a sign of prosperity. Anyone having an overabundance of food will eat to excess and show this in physical stoutness.

In the upper left there is a figure with an elephant's head and six pairs of arms dancing on a shrew, his mount. This is Ganapati, a Buddhist form of the popular Hindu god Ganesha. In this case, too, there is an ambivalence. Ganesha is the Hindu god who clears away obstacles, both spiritual and physical. In Tantric Buddhism there is a school that sees Hindu gods as a hindrance. One of these is the obstacle- or hindrance-remover, Ganesha, who is called Vighna, or obstacle, by

Buddhists. This led to the creation of the Tantric Buddhist divinity Vighnantaka, the "Subduer of Vighna," whereby we see this divinity trample Ganesha underfoot, standing or dancing on him.

Below Ganapati a woman has been painted, standing in tribhanga, the position whereby the body bends sharply twice, thus forming three planes. She is holding onto a tree. This lucky position is known from the earliest depictions of yakshis carved in the stone walls of stupas, such as the great Bharhut and Sanchi stupas, in the second and first century b.c.e. There they symbolize, no differently than in this painting, happiness, prosperity, and the strength to grow.

Opposite her, on the other side of the paubha, sits a man who looks like a Buddhist holy man with a hood of snakes' heads over his head. Presumably he is Nagarjuna, a Southern Indian religious theoretician who reformed Mahayana Buddhism in the second century c.e. (see pages 28 and 29). Nagarjuna is supposed to have obtained his knowledge from the nagas living at the bottom of bodies of water who guarded treasures in the form of knowledge.

Glossary

abhayamudra: "Have No Fear" mudra (see), raised hand with open palm forward.

abhidharma: teachings on metaphysics.

Adi Buddha: the in-dwelling, invisible and formless primeval Buddha, portrayed in art as a white or dark blue buddha with crown and jewels, sometimes referred to as Vajradhara, Vajrasattva, Vajrapani, Mahavairocana, or Samantabhadra. He exists in the dharmakaya (body of the teachings).

ahimsa: compassion toward animals; practicing vegetarianism.

Akshobhya: blue Dhyani Buddha of the cardinal direction east.

alidha: a lunging-to-the-left stance.

All powerful Ten: the symbolism at the heart of the Kalachakra tantra; a mystical symbol written more than 1,000 years ago on the wall of the monastery in Nalanda (Bihar, Northeastern India). Contains the seven letter symbols ya, ra, va, la, ma, ksa, and ha, and the three symbols for sun, moon, and flame.

Amitabha: red Dhyani Buddha of the cardinal direction west; spiritual father of Avalokiteshvara.

Amitayus: crowned form of the dhyani buddha Amitabha.

Amoghasiddhi: green Dhyani Buddha of the cardinal direction north.

amrita: nectar of immortality, symbol of deathlessness of nirvana.

Ananda: a cousin to and favorite student of the Buddha.

anjalimudra: gesture of respectful greeting, palms facing each other in front of the chest.

arhat: "Venerable One," a historical follower of the Buddha, there are sixteen in all who were selected by the Buddha to remain on Earth and protect the teachings. The title for a wise and holy one who, during life, attained nirvana.

arupadhatu: realm of formlessness.

arura: a plum-like medicinal fruit.

Ashoka: Emperor who opened the eight stupas in which the Buddha's cremains were held, and divided them among 84,000 stupas.

ashtamangala: the eight good luck tokens: parasol, fish, treasure urn, lotus, conch shell, wheel, shrivatsa (see), and banner.

Asita: prophet who recognized Siddhartha's supernatural qualities and foretold of his future as a great holy man.

Atisha: founder of the Kadam Order. Brought the Kalachakra Tantra from Bengal to Tibet.

Avalokiteshvara: The Buddha of Compassion, most popular bodhisattva in Mahayana Buddhism. The 108 forms of Avalokiteshvara are grouped under the names "Lokanatha" or "Lokeshvara." Protective deity of Tibet, incarnate as the Dalai Lama

Ayurveda: Ancient Indian system of health care.

Bakula: Oldest of the sixteen Arhats. Also the name of a kind of tree.

Bardo: an intermediary world between death and birth.

Bhavachakra: Wheel of Life.

beggar's bowl: standard attribute of Amitabha, Shakyamuni, and Bhaisajyaguru.

Bhaisajyaguru: Lord of the Lapis Lazuli-Colored Light; Supreme Healer, Lord Who Has a Healing Effect; the most important of the Eight Medicine Buddhas.

bhumisparshamudra: "Calling the Earth to Bear Witness" mudra. A mudra, or hand position in which the right hand rests on the right knee, with the fingertips touching the earth. A common attribute in depictions of the Buddha.

bija: magical syllable connected to a deity's essence.

bindu: center of the universe.

Bodhgaya: city in India where Siddhartha attained enlightenment under the bodhi tree.

bodhicitta: will to enlightenment.

bodhisattvas: divine helpers, beings who have reached enlightenment, but who delay entry into parinirvana in order to help others attain nirvana.

Bön religion: early Tibetan shamanistic religion

Borobudur: name of a famous, eighth-century stupa in Java, Indonesia.

Brahma: Hindu god present at Siddhartha's birth. Recognizable by his four heads.

Brikuti: Nepalese princess who married Songtsen Gampo.

Buddha, the: the enlightened Siddhartha Gautama.

Chakrasamvara: a yidam who strongly resembles Kalachakra; an emantion of Akshobhya, sometimes a form of Hevajra.

chakravartin: "Wheel turner"; a proponent of religious teachings.

Chandraprabha: a bodhisattva, whose name means "Moonlight."

charnel yard: place where corpses are laid to rest before being cremated or processed (as in sky burial).

cintamani: transparent wish stone.

daka: an earth spirit who "eats" whatever is bad for humans.

dakini: "She Who Goes Through the Air;" a type of tantric sorceress who helps believers surmount hindrances.

Dalai Lama: said to be an incarnation of Avalokiteshvara, he is the spiritual leader of Tibet and the leader of the Gelugpa.

Devadatta: Siddhartha's cousin.

dharani: sacred saying, spell

dharma: teachings.

dharmachakra: the wheel of the teachings.

dharmachakramudra: "Setting the Wheel of Teachings into Motion" mudra.

dharmakaya: body of teachings.

dharmapala: fierce guardian of Tibetan Buddhism and its teachings.

Dharmatala: a scholarly layman who served the sixteen arhats during their stay in China. Depicted with a basket full of theological writings on his back; created a tiger from his right knee to protect the arhats.

Dhritarashtra: Lord of the East and of the Heavenly Musicians.

dhyanamudra: "Meditation" mudra.

dhyani buddha: meditation buddha, mystical extension of the Adi Buddha.

Dhyani Buddhas, Five: These are Vairocana, Akshobhya Ratnasambhava, Amitabha, and Amoghasiddhi.

Dorje Drolo (Dorje Trolo): a wrathful manifestion of Padmasambhava, as demon subduer.

double vajra: symbol of wisdom and compassion.

Eightfold Path: right understanding; right intention; right speech; right action; right way of living; right concentration; right effort; right mindfulness.

Ekadashamukha: aspect of Avalokiteshvara with eleven heads.

Five Commandments: not to kill, not to steal, practice of self-control, friendliness, and compassion.

Four Noble Truths: The fundamental teaching of the Buddha: life is suffering; we suffer because of attachments; suffering must stop; suffering may be eliminated by following the Eightfold Path.

gandharvas: heavenly musicians.

Ganges: holy river in Northern India

garuda: a creature with a human body and a bird's head.

Gelugpa (or Gelug Order): "Order of the Virtuous," the most important monastic order in Tibetan Buddhism today. Began in the 14th century. Also known as the "Yellow Hats."

ghanta: bell, prayerbell. Ritual object that symbolizes the female aspect of duality. Together with the vajra, the application of method and wisdom in the resolution of duality.

gonkhang: temple space with protective gods.

Princess Gopi: princess who chose Siddhartha as her marriage partner upon his victory at the tournament.

Green Tara: female bodhisattva that sprung from a tear from Avalokiteshvara's left eye.

Guhyasamaja: a yidam.

Guru Rinpoche: "Precious Teacher," another name by which Padmasambhava is known.

guruparampara: a lineage of teachers; a spiritual family tree.

Heavens of Amitabha, Maitreya, or Skshobhya: popular places to sojourn before being reborn.

Heruka: wrathful yidam deity that is portrayed in yab-yum with their prajna. A fierce, deified form of the yogini.

Hevajra: Buddhist version of the Hindu god Shiva in his guise as Nataraja, King of the Dancers. Also a heruka yidam of the tantra system of the same name. A fierce emanation of Akshobhya.

Hinayana Buddhsim: another term for Theravada Buddhism, meaning "the lesser path."

Hvashang: also spelled Hva-san. A monk who guided the arhats to China. The popular "laughing buddha," or "pot-bellied buddha," known for his generosity.

Indra: King of the Hindu gods, present at Siddhartha's birth; presides over the Heaven of the 33 Gods on Mount Meru.

Jambhala: Buddhist god of wealth.

jambhara fruit: attribute of Jambhala, a type of lemon.

jatakas: stories about the Buddha's previous lives.

ju-i: a scepter that symbolizes happiness and prosperity.

Kadam: order of Tibetan Buddhism that began in the 11th century. Based on the teachings of Atisha, it advocated celibacy and asceticism.

Kagyupa: Tibetan Buddhist order which arose

from the teachings of the mahasiddhas Naropa, Marpa, and Milarepa.

Kalachakra: The favored yidam of the Gelugpa, with four heads, twelve pairs of arms, and one pair of legs, in yab-yum with his consort Vishvamata. Also, The Wheel of Time, a tantra that dates from the 10th century.

kalasha: water jug.

Kamadeva: Hindu god of love.

kamadhatu: realm of wanting.

Kannon: Japanese goddess of compassion.

Kanthaka: the horse that carried Siddhartha, for the last time, away from the royal palace and his life as a prince.

kapala: skull cup.

Kapilavastu: the royal court where Siddhartha spent the first 29 years of his life, and where, as the Buddha, he converted his father to Buddhism.

karma: the manner in which previous lives were lived; sum of one's actions and mental activity.

karuna: compassion.

khakkhara: jingling beggar's staff.

King of Kham: Eastern Tibetan king who was healed by the arhats.

khatvanga: staff.

Kuanyin: Chinese goddess of compassion, often portrayed as a kind of Madonna and Child.

Kushinagara: the city where the Buddha died, at the age of 80.

lama: a scholar of the sutras and tantras of Tibetan Buddhism.

Loden Chogse: "Proclaimer of Wisdom."

Lohan: the Chinese term for the 18 Arhats.

lokapalas: guardians of the cardinal directions.

Lumbini: birthplace, in Southern Nepal, of Siddhartha Guatama.

Madhyamika: formulated by Nagarjuna, this is the Buddhist path of the Middle Way, based on the Prajnaparamita, reconciling the dualism between being and non-being.

Mahakala: "Great Black One," "Great Time," seen holding the Wheel of Life.

Mahasiddha: a great siddha, one who has a lot of siddhi, or spiritual power.

Mahayana Buddhism: "The Great Path" or "The Great Vehicle." Fellow-human-oriented form of Buddhism, beginning at the start of the Christian Era, in which divine helpers, or bodhisattvas, work to help people break through samsara.

Maitreya: a bodhisattva, The Buddha of the Future, who, according to Buddhist tradition, will appear roughly in the year 4500.

mandala: magic circle or ring. A geometric pattern of squares within concentric circles; a projection of the macrocosm.

Mandarava: Indian princess and consort of Padmasambhava

mani: Sanskrit seed vowel, signifying "jewel," signifying the Buddha's teachings

Manjushri: Bodhisattva of Wisdom; counterpart of Hindu god Brahma. Depicted in red, yellow, golden yellow, white, or black; almost always sitting in lotus position, eternally young and muscular; has some 20 variations. An emanation of both the dhyani buddha Amitabha and of Akshobhya.

mantra: : a sacred saying or prayer.

manushi buddha: a mortal incarnation of a bodhisattva.

Mara: personification of evil; the god who tried unsuccessfully to prevent Siddhartha from attaining enlightenment as he meditated under the bodhi tree.

Marpa (1012-1097): Naropa's most well-known Tibetan student. Translated various tantric works into Tibetan. Third patriarch of the Kagyupa. Teacher of Milarepa.

Maudgalyayana: disciple of the Buddha. Sometimes referred to as Mahamaudgalyayana.

Queen Maya: mother of Prince Siddhartha.

Milarepa (1040-1123): student of Marpa who wrote the Gurbum, the "Hundred Thousand Songs," one of the patriarchs of the Kagyupa.

Mount Meru: the cosmic home of the gods, located in the cosmic ocean

mudra: : hand position used in meditation.

muni: a religious sage.

myrobalan plum: a healing fruit used as a laxative or purgative. Often seen in Bhaisajyaguru's hand.

Nagarjuna: southern Indian scholar from the second century c.e., who formulated the Madhyamika (the Middle Way); great theoretician of Mahayana Buddhism.

nakula: a kind of mongoose associated with treasure and wealth.

Nalanda: Buddhist monastic university in Bihar, India.

Nanda: Siddhartha's half-brother.

Naropa (956-1040): student of Tilopa, abbot of Nalanda monastic university. One of the patriarchs of the Kagyupa.

nidanas: twelve links in the cycle of rebirth.

nirmanakaya: the earthly plane of existence.

nirvana: a state of liberation, enlightenment, in which one realizes the way out of the cycle of death, birth, and rebirth.

Nyima Oser: one of the eight guises of Padmasambhava, a siddha who was able to catch rays of sunlight in his hands.

Nyingmapa: "Order of the Elders" established in 1062.

offerings of the five senses: usually two cymbals (sound); one mirror (sight); a silk sash (touch); a shell for burning incense (smell); and fruit (taste).

OM: Sanskrit seed vowel, signifying the cosmic primeval sound that marks the beginning of creation.

OM MANI PADME HUM: a mantra that symbolically encompasses the essence of Buddhism, literally "The Jewel in the Lotus."

108: a sacred number in Buddhism; composed of the powers of the first three numbers, i.e. 1 x 4 x 27 = 108. Buddhist rosaries (mala) often contain 108 beads, or a division of 108 beads.

Padma Gyalpo: also known as Padma Raja, the "Lotus King."

Padmapani: another name for the compassionate buddha Avalokiteshvara. Buddhist counterpart to the Hindu god Brahma.

Padmasambhava: "He Who Was Born from a Lotus;" a manifestation of Avalokiteshvara. He was invited to Tibet by King Trisong Detsen, and succeeded assimilating parts of the Bön religion into Vajrayana Buddhism.

padmasana: lotus position.

padma: lotus; the human heart.

pala: guardians.

Palden Lhamo: fierce tantric goddess of Vajrayana Buddhism; Buddhist version of the Hindu goddess Kali. The protector of Lhasa, the Dalai Lama, and the Panchen Lama.

Panchen Lama: the supreme spiritual authority of Tibetan Buddhism.

parinirvana: passing beyond nirvana.

Parvati: Hindu goddess, Rudra's spouse

pata: precursor of the thangka; a painting of symbols and depictions of deities and saints, primarily found in India.

paubha: a form of the thangka, used by the Buddhist Newari minority in the Katmandu Valley to explain religious principles.

Pemasambha: a wise teacher, one of the eight guises of Padmasambhava.

peris: mountain fairies.

phurbu: magic dagger.

Potala: the Dalai Lama's palace in Lhasa, Tibet. Also the mountain on which Avalokiteshvara resides.

prajna: wisdom; a consort.

Prajnaparamita: Sutra of Transcendental Wisdom, basis of the Yellow Hat Order; also, goddess, personification of knowledge.

pramana: teachings on logic.

pratyeka buddha: someone who has attained personal liberation (as opposed to attaining it for others by teaching and guiding).

Rahulabhadra: one of the sixteen Arhats; son of Siddhartha and Yashodhara.

Rajgir: city where Maudgalyayana, disciple of the Buddha, was purported to have been murdered.

Rati: Kamadeva's spouse.

Ratnasambhava: yellow dhyani buddha of the cardinal direction south.

Red Hats: description of the Tibetan Buddhist Nyingma order.

Rudra: a form of the Hindu god Shiva.

rupadhatu: realm of form.

Sahasrabhuja Lokeshvara: Avalokiteshvara in his thousand-armed aspect.

Sakya: order of Tibetan Buddhism that began in the 11th century.

Samantabhadra: a form of the Adi Buddha; also the name of a bodhisattva.

sambhoga: (spiritual) enjoyment, satisfaction, splendor.

samsara: the cycle of birth, death, and rebirth.

sangha: the monastic community.

sarvabuddha dakini: a type of dakini that has access to all the buddhas, as opposed to dakinis who are affiliated with specific dhyani buddhas.

Second Buddha, The: a title, given by the Nyingma Order, to Padmasambhava.

Second Coming of Buddhism: period in the 11th century when the monastic life began to take root in Tibet.

Senge Dadog: a fierce form of Padmasambhava as dharmapala.

Seven Jewels, The: a frequently-seen element in thangkas; king's and queen's earrings; coral, elephant tusks, rhinoceros horn, cruciform accessory, pearls.

Shadakshari Lokeshvara: an emanation of Avalokiteshvara, Lord of the Six-Syllable Mantra (OM MANI PADME HUM).

Shakyamuni: "enlightened one of the Shakya;" the Buddha Siddhartha Guatama's title when he achieved enlightenment.

Shakyasimha (Shakya Senge): Padmasambhava as the Second Buddha. Lion of the Shakyas.

Shambhala: mythic kingdom in the north of Tibet, in the high, snowy mountains; a paradise on earth which can only be found by people who are sufficiently pure of spirit and free of ignorance.

Shariputra: disciple of the Buddha.

shrivatsa: perpetual knot, symbol of the infinity of Buddhism.

Shuddhodana: Father of Siddhartha Guatama and ruler of the Shakyas, a small tribe in southern Nepal.

shunyata: cosmic emptiness; the Absolute.

Shyamatara: The Green Tara.

siddha: a person who possesses siddhi, nirvana, supernatural powers and qualities that are magically acquired in tantric rites.

Siddhartha Guatama: the Buddha's original birth name.

siddhi: supernatural powers derived from the attainment of nirvana.

Sitatara: name of the White Tara; this goddess represents purity and compassion (as a feminine emanation of Avalokiteshvara).

sky burial: method of burial in Tibet where the body is cut up and given to carrion-eating birds.

King Songtsen Gampo (617-649) unified Tibet and conquered parts of China and Nepal. Fostered Buddhism in Tibet through his marriages to Chinese and Nepalese princesses. Said to be an incarnation of Avalokiteshvara.

stupa: a monument, symbolizing death and rebirth. Originally a dome-shaped burial mound that contained the cremains of holy people; an architectonic three-dimensional rendering of the universe.

Sukhavati Heaven: the Western paradise over which Amitabha presides, popularized with Mahayana Buddhism, and a favored destination for believers.

Suryaprabha: a bodhisattva whose name means "Sunlight."

sutras: religious teachings or sermons.

Svayambhu: Adi Buddha, the "Self-Creating One," who manifested himself as a flame out of the lotus that bloomed from the middle of a lake.

Swat Valley: birth place of Padmasambhava, in the mountainous country of present-day Northern Pakistan.

tantra: literally, "thread." A tantra is a doctrine or ritual system in which everything is interconnected.

Tantrism: pan-Indian movement that is the foundation of many of India's religions.

tara: Buddhist form of the mother goddess, a female bodhisattva. Tara means "star," "savior," "leader."

Tara, Green: female bodhisattva that sprung from a tear from Avalokiteshvara's left eye; also called Shyamatara.

Tara, White: female bodhisattva that sprung from a tear from Avalokiteshvara's right eye, also known as Sitatara.

Tashilunpo Monastery: residence of the Panchen Lama.

terma: "treasures" kept secret by Padmasambhava and his followers.

tertön: "treasure hunters," people with devotion and understanding proper to the discovery of terma (see).

thangka: literally, "something that can be rolled up." A painting used as a religious aid in ritual actions, as a guideline and help in meditation, and for protection and healing.

Theravada Buddhism: original Buddhism, "The Doctrine of the Elders," also called Hinayana Buddhism, in which people seek their own, individual nirvana.

Three Jewels, the: the triratna, essential to the continuity of the Buddhist teachings—the Buddha, the dharma, and the sangha.

Tiger's Lair: Taksang Monastery in the Paro Valley, Bhutan.

Tilopa (928-1009): one of the mahasiddhas, guru to Naropa; abbot of Odantapura monastery.

Trayastrimsha Heaven: the Heaven of the 33 Gods, where the Buddha went to teach his mother, Queen Maya.

Tree of Refuge: a portrayal of a lineage of spiritual teachers.

tribhanga: a position in which the body makes two sharp bends, forming three axis on top of one another.

trikaya: "three bodies" concerning the three realms or levels in which or on which a buddha manifests—adi buddha, dhyani buddha, and manushi buddha.

tripitaka: the Buddha's canon, literally meaning "the three baskets," as the collected texts were kept in three baskets. They contained rules for monastic life, sutras, and jatakas.

triratna: "The Three Jewels:" the Buddha, the dharma (the Buddha's teachings), and the sangha (the monastic community).

Trisong Detsen (755-797): King of Tibet who brought Padmasambhava to his court in order to promote Vajrayana Buddhism.

Tsongkhapa (1357-1419): founder of the Gelug monastic order (Gelugpa). Honorific title is Je Rinpoche. Born in Amdo, Eastern Tibet, in the Onion Valley. Considered to be an earthly incarnation of Manjushri; was retroactively designated as the first Dalai Lama.

tulkus: enlightened incarnations of religious predecessors.

Tushita Heaven: Maitreya's paradise.

upaya: method

ushnisha: fontanel bulge signifying special mental capacities.

Ushnishavijaya: a goddess, revered in Nepal, with three heads and eight arms; Mother of All Buddhas; incarnation of Sitatara.

Vairocana: white dhyani buddha of the cardinal direction center.

Vaishravana: guardian of the North, Lord of the yakshas, Buddhist version of Kubera.

vajra: symbol of Vajrayana Buddhism; "diamond," also thunder-dagger or wedge; a ritual object; bolt of lightning; originally in Hinduism the weapon belonging to Indra, god of rain, thunder, and lightning; symbolizes the male aspect of duality.

Vajrabhairava: one of the many fierce guises of Manjushri.

Vajrapani: Buddhist counterpart of Hindu god Indra; his name derives from the vajra.

Vajrasattva: An adi buddha.

Vajrayana Buddhism: the most well-known form of Tantric Buddhism, developed from Mahayana Buddhism. Here, the practitioner works on the self to attain non-duality and personal union with the All.

Varamudra: "Giving or Granting" mudra. Gesture of granting favor and offering material and spiritual gifts.

Varanasi: Modern-day Benares, near Sarnath, where the Buddha began to teach.

Vikramashila: Buddhist monastic university.

vinaya: monastic rules.

Virudhaka: Guardian of the South, Lord of the Giants.

Virupaksha: Guardian of the West, Lord of the Nagas.

Vishnu: protective Hindu god who oversees creation.

Vishvamata: Consort of Kalachakra, and Mother of All.

Vitarkamudra: the gesture of giving instruction for believers.

Wen-che'ng: T'ang princess, niece of the emperor, who married Songtsen Gampo and installed a jobo (gilt figure of Shakyamuni Buddha) in the Jo-Khang Temple, Lhasa's most important shrine.

Xuan Zang: famous Chinese monk who left the T'ang capital Xi'an in 629 for India, traveled through the Takla Makan Desert and Karakoram Range in order to collect Buddhist writings and visit holy places. Carried out the translation of these writings in the Wild Goose Pagoda.

yab-yum: "man-woman;" image of the sexual embrace in which male and female divinities in Tibetan thangkas are frequently seen; representing the reconciliation of polarities and duality; an important aspect of Tantric Buddhism.

yaksha: earth spirit.

Yama: god of hell, one of the eight dharmapalas, ruler of the south who rides a water buffalo.

Yami: Yama's sister and consort.

Yamantaka: a yidam, "Subduer of Yama." fierce manifestation of Manjushri and Akshobhya.

Yamuna: holy river in Northern India.

yana: "path."

Yashodhara: Siddhartha's second wife, who bore his son, Rahula.

Yellow Hat Order: the Gelugpa, currently the most important monastic order of Tibetan Buddhism.

Yeshe Tsogyal: Padmasambhava's student and wife who wrote the his biography, the *Pemakathang*.

yidam: personal guardian deities associated with specific tantras; personification of a tantra system such as the Kalachakra Tantra or the Hevajra Tantra. An archetype; as a fierce energy, it represents one's own spiritual force confronting obstacles; a portrayal of the believing self.

Yogacara School: the second great Mahayana philosophy which was carried through in Vajrayana Buddhism, based on yoga and meditation. Developed between the third and fifth centuries c.e.

yogapatta: a strap used in meditation to prevent one's legs from falling to the side.

yogi: male practitioner of yoga.

yogini: female yogi.

Yoga: "linking;" the practice of uniting body and spirit with the cosmos.

Bibliography

Brauen, Martin. *The Mandala: Sacred Circle in Tibetan Buddhism*. Martin Willson, trans. Boston: Shambhala, 1998.

Dagyab Rinpoche and Loden Sherab. *Tibetan Religious Art*. Wiesbaden, 1977.

Dagyab Rinpoche, Loden Sherab, and Robert Thurman. *Buddhist Symbols in Tibetan Culture: An Investigation of the Nine Best-Known Groups of Symbols*. Maurice Walshe, trans. Somerville, MA: Wisdom Publications, 1995.

Essen, Gerd-Wolfgang, and Tsering Tashi Thingo. *Die Götter des Himalaya: Buddhistische Kunst Tibets*. Munich: Prestel, 1989.

Evans-Wentz, W.Y. *Tibet's Great Yogi Milarepa. A Biography from the Tibetan being the Jetsün-Kahbum*. London: Oxford University Press, 1928.

Fisher, Robert E. *Art of Tibet*. London: Thames & Hudson, 1997.

Jackson, David P., and Janice A. Jackson. *Tibetan Thangka Painting: Methods and Materials*. Illustrated by Robert Beer. Ithaca: Snow Lion, 1988.

Lauf, Detlef-Ingo. *Secret Revelation of Tibetan Thangkas. Verborgene Botschaft Tibetischer Thangkas*. Freiburg im Breisgau, 1976.

Linrothe, Rob. *Ruthless Compassion: Wrathful Deities in Early Indo-Tibetan Esoteric Buddhist Art*. Boston: Shambhala, 1999.

Pott, P. H. *Yoga and Yantra: Their Interrelation and Their Significance for Indian Archeology*. The Hague, 1966.

Rhie, Marylin M., and Robert A. F. Thurman. *Wisdom and Compassion: The Sacred Art of Tibet*. Photographs by John Bigelow Taylor. New York: Tibet House/Harry N. Abrams, 1996; Abradale Press/Harry N. Abrams, 2000.

Tucci, G. *Tibetan Painted Scrolls*. (3 vols.) Rome: La Libreria dello Stato, 1949; Bangkok digital reprint from slides of Tucci's originals, 1999.

Index

abhayamudra, 22, 24
abhidharma, 71
abundance, symbols of,
  86
Adi Buddha, 17, 43, 22,
  52, 54, 69, 73, 76
Akshobhya, 22, 24, 41,
  76
  fierce emanation of,
    76
  Heaven of, 64
alidha, 54
All-powerful Ten Man-
  dala, 82, 83
Amdo, 71
Amitabha, 18, 21, 22, 24,
  38, 43, 43, 46, 52, 54,
  64, 71
Amitayus, 46
Amoghasiddhi, 22, 24
amrita, 41, 49, 72, 85
Ananda, 18, 20
Aniko, ix
animal hide, 59, 63
anjalimudra, 38
antelope hide, 38
arhat, 18, 21, 34, 35, 37,
  47
Arhats, Eighteen, 35, 36
arms, idea of a thousand,
  41
arupadhatu, 82
arura, 34
Arya, 7
ashtamangala, 26
Asita, 8, 10
Ashoka, 16
Atisha, 49, 71, 73
Aum, 38
aureole, 41, 52
  flaming, 54, 73, 72
Avalokiteshvara, x, 21,
  24, 37-38, 38, 41, 43,
  46, 52, 66, 71, 72, 82
Ayurveda, 30

banner, 28, 86
Bakula, 34
Bardo, 64-66, 76
Bardo Thödol, 49
baskets, three, 17
bat, 35

begging for food, 18, 59
  beggar's bowl, 18, 30,
    63
  beggar's staff, 20, 49
behavior, irreligious, 30
Being and Non-Being, 71
Bhaisajyaguru, x, 18, 30,
  31, 34
bhakti movement, 21
Bharhut stupa, 88
bhavachakra, 30, 64, 69
bhumisparshamudra, 18,
  22, 24, 26
Bhumi, 85
Bhutan, 49, 52
Bihar, 57
bija, 80
bindu, 82
birth, 66
Black Hat Sorcerers, 71
Blind old man, 66
bo tree, 14
bodhi, 21, 73
  tree, 12
bodhicitta, 22
bodhisattva, 2, 21, 24,
  38, 43, 54, 66
  of Knowledge, 71
  of Wisdom, 41
bodhisattvas, 21, 22, 35,
  37, 43, 47, 69
Bodhgaya, 12, 14
bodily fluids, three, 30
body heat, 61
Bön religion, 49, 54, 63
book, 35, 41, 71
  of Wisdom, 85
bow and arrow, 41
bowl, 63
  of offerings, 46
Brahman, 34
  Brahmans, 7, 20
Brahma, 8, 41, 46, 73
brains, 54
British Younghusband
  expedition, 41
Brikuti, 43
bride, 66
Buddha, the, 7-18, 24,
  28, 34, 38, 54, 63, 66,
  66, 85

with Dhyani Buddhas,
  23
life of the, 9, 11, 13,
  15
buddha, 2, 46
  emanations of a, 22
  family, 76
  figures, worship of, 49
  of the Future, 21, 69
  historic, 24, 41, 47
  medicine, 33
  new, 24
  next, coming of 34
  pot-bellied laughing
    buddha, 37
  buddhas, 35 confes-
    sional, 28,69
  buddhas, medicine,
    28-35
  buddhas, series of 24,
    25, 26, 27, 29
buddhahood, 38
  individual, 47
Buddhism, 7, 57
  demise of in India, 49
  growth of number of
    buddhas in, 24
  message of, 59
  northern, 20
  symbol of, 28
Buddhist holy man, 88
Burma, 18
burial mound, 12
butcher's knife, 54

Calling the Earth to Bear
  Witness mudra, 22, 24
caste system, 7, 14
cardinal direction, 80
  cardinal directions,
    guardians of, 69
  four, 28, 30
caricatures, 37
celestials, 86
chakra, 8, 14, 28, 73, 82
Chakrasamvara, 69, 75
  76
chakravartin, 8
Chandraprabha, 34
chariots, 80
charnel grounds, eight,
  80

charnel yard, 52, 54, 57,
  80
Chenrezi, x
children, 37
China, 1, 35, 37
Chinese
  annexation of Tibet, ix
  art, 35

  conventions, formal,
    37
  Cultural Revolution,
    ix
  emperor, 35, 37
  iconography, 37, 35
  longevity symbols, 41
  Madonna and Child,
    37
  style, 34, 35
Chobar, 43
cintamani, 38
civet, 86
Clad in Cotton, 61
cleaver, 54
clouds, 35
cobra, 86
commandments, five, 18
compassion, 18, 21, 37,
  37, 43, 46, 52
conch, 28, 86
conch shell, 28
Confessional Buddha, 28
coral, 35, 38, 63
cosmic ocean, 69
cosmic realm, 22
  cosmic primeval
    sound, 38
couple, loving , 66
commissioners, 85
cremation grounds, 54, 57
crown, 35, 63, 76
cruciform accessory, 38
cymbals, 46

daka, 35
dakini, 2, 54
  link between earthly
    and supernatural,
    54
  dakinis, 54, 69
Dalai Lama, 38, 71, 72,
  damaru, 52

dangers, eight great, 46
darkness, 41, 80
dancers, 85
dead person, 66
death, 49
death's-heads, five small, 76
deer, 35, 41
deities
  with animal heads, 76
  concentration on, 47
  division into ranks, 69
  Hindu, 73
  terrifying, 80
  wrathful, 54, 76
demon subduer, 52
demons, 46, 54
desire, 52
Devadatta, 10, 20
Dharamsala, x
dharani, 47, 80
dharma, 14, 18, 34, 38, 46, 52, 85
dharmachakra, 41
dharmachakras, eight, 80
dharmachakramudra, 22, 24, 72
dharmakaya, 22, 49, 52, 69
dharmapala, 2, 43, 52, 69, 72, 80
dharmapalas, 41, 80
Dharmatala, 37
Dhritarashtra, 73
dhyanamudra, 22, 24
dhyanasana, 22
dhyani bodhisattvas, 24
dhyani buddha, 22, 24, 30, 54, 54, 82
Dhyani Buddhas, Five, 22, 34
  and female partners, 43
  fierce forms, 76
diamond, 47
directions, four intermediary , 28
disk-shaped weapon, 28
divine element, return of, 21
divine seed inside the body, 22
divinities, amalgamations of Buddhist and Hindu, 37
divinities, yab-yum, 47

divinity, primary, 2
Doctrine of the Elders, 18, 21
dorje, x
Dorje Drolo, 52
Drepung, 71
drinking goblet, 76
Drukpa, 49
drum of two skulls, 76
dualistic view of being and non-being, 28
duality, elimination of, 73
dwarves, pot-bellied, 85

eagle feather, 52
  eagles, 34
earlobes, 35, 17
earrings, king's and queen's, 35, 38, 63
ears, 54
earth spirit, 35
  earth spirits, male and female, 85
earth goddess, 14, 85
ego, banishment of, 80
eight tokens of good luck, 18
eight compass points, 28
Eightfold Path, 18, 21
Eight Medicine Buddhas, 28, 30
84,000, 8, 16
Ekadashamukha, 38
elephant, 69, 86
  white, 8
  tusks, 35, 38, 63
  elephants, 8, 46
eleven-headed aspect of Avalokiteshvara, 38
embrace of man and woman, 47
emptiness, 47, 73
  cosmic, 17
energy channels, three vertical, 49
enlightenment, 7, 24
  opportunity for, 54
entrance gates, 80
eras of human existence on Earth, five, 22
European position, 16
events, extraordinary 7, 16
evergreen, 35
evil spirits, 30
exorcism, 57

extinction, 66, 82
eye, arrow in, 66
  eye located in the palms, 41
  eyes, 54

failings, three major, 52
fairytale, German, 86
feeling, 46
female bodhisattvas and goddesses, 47
fertility, 8, 86
fingers, three raised, 46
fire, 46
  ring of, 80
  in Tantrism, 80
fish, 26
  fish, gold, 57
five elements, 30
five senses, sacrifice of, 80
  fierce-deity variety, 80
flame, 43, 82
  flames, 52
flayed husband, 41
fly whisk, 35, 37
food, improper, 30
fortune, symbol of, 26
four encounters, 7, 10-12
Four Great Kings, 73
Four Noble Truths, 14
fruits, 46
  picking, 66

Ganapati, 88
Ganden, 71
gandharvas, 73
Ganges, 26
garuda, 85, 86
Gathering of Saints, 66, 68
Ganesha, 88
Gelug Order (see also Gelugpa), 49
  appearance of, 49
  assimilation of the Kadam Order, 49
  founder of, 71
Gelugpa, x, 69, 72
  abbots, 72
  absorption of Kadampa, 71
  foundation of, 71
  founder of, 43
  hereditary successors in, 71
  and line of reincarna-

tion, 71
  yidam of, 73
gem, glowing 36
generosity, 37
gesture of
  respectful greeting, 38
  giving, 46, 85
  giving instruction, 41
  granting favor, 41, 85
  offering material and spiritual gifts, 43
Giving or Granting mudra, 22, 24
gnome, 35, 85-86
god of love, 73
goddess, horrifying, 41
  goddess of happiness and prosperity, 85
gonkhang, 76
good luck symbols, 26, 30, 35, 38
Great Black One, 66
Great Exodus, 35
great path, 21
Great Perfect One, 57
Great Time, 66
great vehicle, 21
Great Wild Goose Pagoda, 37
Green Tara, 45, 46
griffin-like creature, 86
guardians
  of the cardinal directions, 73
  of the north, 73, 86
  of the teachings, 41, 52, 72
  of the treasures of the earth, 86
  of the South, 73
Guhyasamaja, 69
Gurbum, 61
guru, 47, 49, 52, 54
  gurus, 2, 52, 59, 69, 71
Guru Rinpoche, 50, 54
  hidden wrathfulness, 49
guruparampara, 66

half-moon, 86
hand positions, 47
happiness, 88
  and prosperity, 35
hat, 49, 52
hatred, 52

Have No Fear mudra, 22, 24
He Vajra, 76
He Who Was Born from a Lotus, 49
head, elephant's, 88
heads, animal, 86
    heads, lions', 86
    heads, elephants', 86
    heads, three, 54
hearing, 46
Heaven of 33 Gods, 16, 35, 69
heruka, 73, 76, 77
Hevajra, 69, 73
    as Akshobhya, 73
Hevajra Tantra, 72
Hilton, James, 82
Himalayas, x, 49, 30, 86
Hinayana, 21
Hindu god of wealth, 73
Hinduism, 7, 8, 14, 49, 57
    early, 47
    eight mother goddesses in, 46
holy man, false, 20
homeopathic materia medica, 30
hood of snakes' heads, 88
horseback riders, Mongolian, 73
house, 66
HUM, 38
Hundred Thousand Songs, 59, 61
hungry spirits, kingdom of, 64
Hvashang, 37

ignorance, 34, 52
illness, 30
immortality nectar, 46
incarnation, mortal, 24
incense, 46
    burner, 35
    offerings, 28
India, ix, 1, 30, 37, 49, 59
    Northern, 7, 14, 26
    plagued by invading Moslems, 49
Indian
    medicine, ancient 30
    painting, 34
    style, 34

tradition, 37
Indra, 8, 16, 46, 47, 69
initiation goddesses, 54
intestines, 76
ishtadevata, x
Islam, 7

Jainism, 14
Japan, ix, 37
Jambhala, 35, 73, 85, 86, 88
jambhara fruit, 35
jatakas, 17, 24
Java, 80
Je Rinpoche, 71
jewel, 38
    flaming, 73
    jewels, 63, 85, 88
    string of 36
jewelry, 34, 46, 54
jina, 22
jobo, 43
Jo-khang Temple, 43
ju-i, 35

Kadam Order, x, 48-49
    founder of, 71
Kagyu Order (Kagyupa), 49, 59
    patriarchs of, 59
kala, 66, 73
    and chakra, 73
Kalachakra, 72, 73
    initiations, 73
    Mandala, 80, 81, 82
    rites, 82
    tantra, 72, 73, 82
    origins, 73
kalasha, 41
Kali, 41
Kamadeva, 72
kamadhatu, 82
Kannon, 37
Kanthaka, 12
kapala, 49, 54
Kapilavastu, 12, 16
Karakoram Range, 37
karma, 7, 21, 54, 59, 64, 66, 85
    negative, 14, 30
    karmas, bad, 64
    karmas, good, 64
Karmapa, 49
karuna, 37
Kashmir, 1, 49
Kathmandu, ix

Valley, 1, 43, 85
Kham, King of, 34
khakkhara, 49
khatvanga, 49, 54
King of the Dancers, 73
Kipling, Rudyard, 86
knowledge, 71
    three major forms, 64
Kuanyin, 37
Kubera, 73, 85
    as yaksha, 86
kumbhandas, 73
Kushinagara, 16

Ladakh, 1, 49
lake, 41, 46, 49, 69
lakshanas, 8, 10
Lakshmi, 85
lama, 49, 69
Lamaism, 49
landscape
    meaning, 41, 43
    stylized, 59
    Tibetan, 59
Langdarma, 1
lalitasana, 86
left side as female, 41
Lhasa, 38, 41
    British presence in, 41
liberation, 14, 16, 18, 21, 80
    from samsara, 64
life is suffering, 14
Line of Teachers, 66
lion mask, 85
lion, rearing, 86
Lion of the Shakyas, 52
lions, 46
lives, former, 64
Loden Chogse, 52
logic, 71
Lohan, 35
Lokanatha, 37
lokapala, 2, 73
    lokapalas, four, 69
Lokeshvara ("Lord of the World"), 37
longevity, symbols of, 35
Lord
    of the East, 73
    of Giants, 73
    of the Heavenly Musicians, 73
    of the Lapis Lazuli-Colored Light, 30
    of the Nagas, 73

of the Six-Syllable Mantra, 38
of the West, 73
Who Has a Healing Effect, 30
of the Yakshas, 73
Lost Horizon, 82
lotus, 26, 37, 38, 41, 43, 46, 49, 69, 71, 73, 85, 86
    blue, 43
    King, 52
    lake, 52
    with multicolored petals, 86
    petal, 41
    petals, circle of, 80
    pillow, 46
    position, 63
    represents human heart, 38
    symbol of immaculacy, 26
    white, 43
lucky charms, 34, 41
lucky numbers, 26
Lumbini, 7, 8

Madhyamika (the Middle Way), 28, 69, 71
maggots, 63
magic, 57
    dagger, 73
    sayings, 47
    staff, 49
magicians, 47
Mahakala, 66
Mahamaudgalyayana, 20
mahasiddha, 54, 57, 59, 63-64
    deviant behavior of, 59
    features of, 59
    paranormal abilities, 57
Mahatma Gandhi, 14
Mahavairocana, 22
Mahayana Buddhism, 20, 21, 28, 46, 47, 88
    bodhisattvas, two kinds of in 21
    influence of Hindu elements on, 46
    monasteries, 21
    opportunity for popular belief, 21

parallelism with the
practice of Hin-
duism, 21
philosophy, 28
series of buddhas, 21
Maitreya, 21, 24, 69
Heaven of, 64
makaras, 86
Manali, x
mandala, 52, 69, 76, 80
basis of the painted,
82
as cosmogram, 80
in initiation rites, 80
as a projection of the
cosmos, 76
as psychogram, 80
of Yama, 78, 79, 80
Mandarava, 49, 52
mandorla, 20
MANI, 38
Manjushri, 21, 34, 41,
42, 43, 43, 46, 52, 71,
80, 82
body, muscular, 38
book as attribute, 34
dual origin, 43
emanation of Amitab-
ha, 43
and goddess Prajna-
paramita, 41
twenty variations, 43
as Yamantaka, 80
man, scantily clad 36
Man-la, x
mantra, 26, 38, 47, 72
manushi buddha, 22, 24
Mara's attack, 7, 14
Mara's evil forces, 18
Mara's daughters, 14
Marpa, 59, 63
married status, 61
return to Tibet, 61
Marpa's scroll, 61, 63
Maudgalyayana, 18, 20,
28
medicine buddha, x, 35,
30
meditation, 28, 59, 80
buddha, 22
on dhyani buddha, 22
mudra, 24, 22
position, 18
techniques, 47
meditator, physical hall-
marks of a, 18

metaphysics, 71
microcosm and macro-
cosm, 47, 80, 82
Middle Way, 14, 71
Milarepa, 59, 60, 61, 61,
63
miracles, 8
mirror, 46, 52
moksha, 14
monasteries, 30
entrances of, 64, 73
monastery, 52
monastic
borrowing of saints,
71
life, Tibetan, 49
monastic order, 14,
18, 20, 71
rules, 71
mongoose, 34, 86
monk, 18, 24, 34, 35, 49,
52, 54, 57, 59, 69
monk's clothing, 18
monkey, 66
Moon, 49, 82, 86
Mother of All, 73
Mother of All Buddhas,
46
Mount Meru, 69, 80, 82
mountain, 69, 86
mudra, 18, 47
Muhammadanism, 49
mule, 41
muni, 7
murals, 30
mushroom, long-life, 35
musicians, 85
Mussoorie, x
myrobalan plum, 30

Nag, 86
nagas, 87, 88
green, 86
Nagarjuna, 28, 88
nakedness, 54
nakula, 34, 35, 86, 88
Nalanda monastery, 49,
59, 82
Nanda, 10
Naropa, 57, 58, 59, 61,
73
Nataraja, 73
necklace of skulls, 76
nectar of immortality, 41,
49, 85, 86
Nepal, ix, 1, 37, 46, 49

southern, 7
nettle soup, 63
Newari, ix, 1, 85
nidanas, 66
nimbus, 20
nirmanakaya, 24, 49, 54,
69
nirvana, 14, 18, 21, 24,
34, 47, 49, 54, 64, 72
attained in full health
and well-being, 14
deathlessness of 43
state, 22
Noble Eightfold Path, 14
non-dualism, 47
nose, 54
number 108, 38
number 35, 28
numerologists, 28
nuns, 18, 20, 54
Nyingma Order
(Nyimgmapa), 49, 49,
69
Nyima Oser, 52

O Vajra, 76
ocean, 57
cosmic, 80
Odantapura, 57
offering, five-senses, 46,
54
fierce-deity variety, 54
OM, 38
OM MANI PADME
HUM, 26, 38
Onion Valley, 71
Order of Elders, 49
Order of the Virtuous, 71

Padma Gyalpo, 52
Padma Raja, 52
Padmapani, 37, 46
feminine appearance,
37
emanation of Amitab-
ha, 37
Padmasambhava, 41, 46,
49, 49, 54, 63, 69, 71
birth, mysterious
nature of, 49, 52
eight guises of, 52, 53
fierce form of, 52
heroism, magical feats
of, 49
and magic arts, 49
Mystical, 49, 51

as the Second Buddha,
49, 52
padmasana, 63
PADME, 38
painting, religious 85
pala, 52
Palden Lhamo, 41, 80
palm leaf, 41
Panchen Lama, 71, 82
paradise on earth, 82
prospect of heavenly,
21
parasol, 18, 26
parinirvana, 7, 21
Paro Valley, 52
Parvati, 72
patas, 1
path, 47
to bodhi, 38
to liberation, 64
paubha, 1, 85, 88
pauper's bible, 64
peaches, 35
peacock, 34
feather, 52
medicinal context, 34
pearls, 35, 38
Pemakathang, 49
people, two in a boat, 66
peris, 54
perpetual knot, 28
phurbu, 72
pig, black, 64
plants, poisonous 34
plants, medicinal 30
poison, 52
polarities, 47
Potala, 38
potter, 66
prajna (consort), 17
prajna, 28, 38, 73, 76, 80
feminine characteris-
tic, 28
Prajnaparamita, 28, 41,
71
pramana, 71
pratyeka buddha, 18, 21,
47
prayer beads, 38
prayer wheel, 26
Precious Teacher, 49
priests, 28
primeval Buddha, 22
Princess Gopi, 10
prisons, 46

proclaiming the teach-
    ings, 7, 14
Proclaimer of Wisdom,
    52
prosperity, 88
purity, 43

Queen Maya, 8, 16
    Queen Maya's dream,
    7-8
Queen Victoria, 41
quintuple system, 22

Rajgir, 20
Rahula (Rahulabhadra),
    35
ram's horn, 59
Rati, 72
Ratnasambhava, 22, 24
rebirth, 14, 64, 66
red, 54
Red Hats, 71
reincarnation, 14, 21, 64
    cycle of, 7
religious cure, 30
Repa, 61
rhinoceros horn, 38, 63
rice, sheaf of ripe, 85
Rig Veda, 80
right side as the male
    side, 41
Rikki-Tikki-Tavi, 86
rites, tantric, 57
ritual actions, 47
river, 57, 86
robes, 35
rocks, 35, 43
rooster, red, 64
rosary, 85
Rudra, 72
rules for monastic life, 17
rupadhatu, 82

Sahasrabhuja Lokeshvara,
    38, 40, 41
saints, 47
Sakya Order, 49
salvation, 47
Samantabhadra, 17, 22
sambhoga, 22
sambhogakaya, 22, 49,
    54, 69
samsara, 7, 10, 14, 18,
    38, 54, 57, 66, 80
Sanchi, 88

sangha, 18, 46, 85
Sanskrit, x
Sarnath, 14, 28
sarvabuddha
    dakini, 54
    Yogini, 55
sattva, 21
scepter, 35
Second Coming of Bud-
    dhism, 1, 49
seeing, 46
Self-Creating One, 43
Senge Dadog, 52
Sera, 71
sermons, 17
Setting the Wheel of
    Teachings into Motion
    mudra, 22, 24
Seven Jewels, 35, 38, 63
sexual embrace, 54
seven letter symbols, 82
Shadakshari Lokeshvara,
    38, 39, 38, 41
Shakya, 20
Shakyamuni, x, 7, 14, 16,
    17, 18, 22, 24, 26, 28,
    34, 43, 46, 47, 69, 71,
    82
    epithet for, 52
    honorific title for, 22
    period of, 24
    with Shariputra and
        Maudgalyayana, 19
    sixteen disciples of, 34
    as spiritual healer, 30
    34 component factors,
        28
    as ur-physician, 30
Shakya Senge, 52
Shakyas, 7
Shakyasimha, 52
shamanism, Central
    Asian, 54
Shambhala, 82
Shangri-La, 82
Shariputra, 18, 20, 28, 35
    and Maudgalyayana,
        26
She Who Goes through
    the Air, 54
shell, 46, 86
Shiva, 72, 80
Shri, 85
Shridevi, 41
Shrivatsa, 28

Shuddhodana, 7, 10
shunyata, 17, 22, 47, 49,
    64, 69, 73
Shyamatara, 46
siddha, 52, 57
Siddhartha Gautama, 7,
    14, 24, 35
    asceticism of, 7, 12-14
    birth of 7, 8
    enlightenment of, 14
    leaves the palace, 7, 12
    his life at the court, 7,
        10
    parinirvana, 16

raising the young
    prince, 7, 8, 10
    prominence, 24
siddhi, 54, 57
Sikkim, 49
silk sash, 46
sins, three major, 64
Sitatara, 43, 46
    manifestation of Aval-
        okiteshvara, 43
    incarnation of, 46
skull, 57, 76
    the top of, 54
    cup, 49, 52, 73
    skulls, three 50
sky burial, 54
smelling, 46
snakes, 46, 85, 86, 87
    and fertility, 86
    green, 64
    guardians of treasures,
        86
    poisonous, 41, 34
    Southern Asian atti-
        tude regarding, 86
snow leopard, 73, 86
son of Siddhartha, 35
Songtsen Gampo, x, 1, 43
    death of, 49
    incarnation of Aval-
        okiteshvara, 43
sorceress, 54
spells, 47, 57
spiritual leaders, 2
    spiritual power, 26
    spiritual sleep, 52
Srong Tsen Ganpo, x
staff, 49, 73, 76
stance, lunging to the
    left, 54

strength, 46, 52, 88
stupa, 12, 16, 76, 78, 80,
    88
    Borobudur, 80
    Bharhut, 88
    miniature, 35
    Sanchi, 88
    of Svayambhunath, 43
    as symbol of escaping
        samsara, 80
    as three-dimensional
        rendering of the
        universe, 76
Subduer of Vighna, 88
Subduer of Yama, 80
suffering, Buddha's teach-
    ing on, 28
    suffering, cessation of,
        14
Sukhavati Heaven, 21, 46
Sun, 49, 82, 86
    symbol, 28
Supreme Healer, 30
supreme teacher, 2
Suryaprabha, 34
Sutra of Transcendental
    Wisdom, 28
sutras, 17
Svayambhu, 43
Swat Valley, 49, 54
sword, 34, 43, 71
    flaming, 41

Takla Makan Desert, 37
Taksang Monastery, 52
Tamang, ix
T'ang capital Xi'an, 37
T'ang emperor, 43
tantra, 47
    four categories, 69
tantras, 63
    path of, 64
Tantric Buddhism, 20,
    22, 41, 52, 49, 73, 57,
    88
    school that sees Hindu
        gods as a hin-
        drance, 88
    Tantric deities, 85
    tantric goddess, 41
Tantrism, 47, 49, 54, 54
Tara, 43
    as mother goddess, 46
    Green, 35, 41, 43, 45,
        46, 52, 82

White, 41, 43, 44, 43, 82
Tashilunpo Monastery, 71
tasting, 46
tathagata, 22
    attribute of, 43
terma, 49
tertön, 49
Thailand, 18
thangka,
    appreciation for, ix
    curative effect, 30
    framing, 5
    function, ix, 1, 47
    how made, 2-5
    sketching, 3
    medicinal, 30, 32
    painters, Nepalese, 73
    painting 3-5
    preparation of founda-
        tion, 2
    theme and composi-
        tion, 1-2
Theravada Buddhism, 18,
    20, 21, 47, 57, 63
35 Confessional Buddhas,
    26, 69
Thor, 47
thousand-buddha wall,
    24, 26
Three Jewels, 18, 85
throne, 86
thrones, Bengal, 86
thumb and forefinger, 46
thunderbolt, 46, 47
thunder-dagger, x, 47
Tibet, 28, 30, 43, 49, 59,
    82
    Eastern, 71
    and international
        political stage, 43
    medical knowledge in,
        30
    protective diety of, 38
Tibetan
    art, Chinese influences
        in, 59
    Book of the Dead, 49
    Buddhism, 1, 46
    Buddhists, 38
    medicine, 30
    painting, 35, 37
    writing, 28
Tibetans, 49
tiger, 37, 35

Tiger's Lair, 52
tigress, pregnant, 52
Tilopa, 54, 56, 57, 59, 61
time, 66
tongue, 54
tourists, ix
toxins, three major, 52
Trayastrimsha Heaven, 16
treasure pot, 26
treasure and wealth, 34
tree, symbolism in Asia,
    69
tree branch, woman
    grasps a, 8, 88
Tree of Refuge, 71
trees, green, 86
triangle, 73
tribhanga position, 34, 88
trident, 54
trikaya, 22
tripitaka, 17
triratna, 18, 46, 49, 63
Trisong Detsen, 1, 49, 49
trumpet, sound of, 28
Tsongkhapa, 43, 70, 71,
    71
Tucci, Giuseppe, ix
tulkus, 69
Tushita Heaven, 69
Twelve-Part Causality
    Series, 64

underworld, 64
universities, Buddhist, 49
upaya, 52, 73, 76
urn, 85, 86
ushnisha, 10, 17
Ushnishavijaya, 46

Vairocana, 22, 24
Vaishravana, 73, 73
vajra, x, 46, 47, 49, 52,
    54
    double, 49
    family, 76
    and ghanta, 73, 80
    vajras, circle of, 80
Vajrabhairava, 43
Vajradhara, 22
Vajra Heruka, 76
Vajrapani, 21, 22, 46, 52,
    82
    demonic guises, 46
    demonic head of, 38
    protection from possi-

ble dangers, 46
Vajrasattva, 76, 22
Vajrayana Buddhism, 28,
    47, 49, 73
    demonic figures in, 73
    development in Tibet,
        63
    basic principles, 47
    practice of in Tibet, 49
varamudra, 22, 24, 41,
    43, 46, 85
Varanasi (Benares), 14
Vasudhara, 85, 86, 87
Vedas, 41
Vedic priests, 7
Vedism, 7
Vighna, 88
Vighnantaka, 88
Vikramashila, 49
vinaya, 71
Virudhaka, 73
Virupaksha, 73
Vishnu, fierce form of, 80
Vishvamata, 72
vitarkamudra, 41

water, 35, 46
    bottle, 37
    buffalo, 80, 80
    creatures, 86
    jug, 41
weasel, 86
Wen-che'ng, 43
Western Paradise, 64
wheel, 28, 73
    of Life, 61, 65, 64, 67
    of rebirth, 7
    spinning, 64
    of teachings, 14, 43,
        80
    of Time, 73
White Tara, 41, 43, 44,
    46
wish fulfillment, 26
wish stone, 38
wisdom, 38, 46, 52, 73
    and compassion, 46
woman handing man
    drink, 66
woman, pregnant, 66
world
    of the demigods, 66
    four corners of, 80
    of giants, 66
    of the gods, 66

of humans, 66
period, 24

Xuan Zang, 37

yab-yum, 52, 72, 73, 76
yaksha, 35, 85, 86, 88
yakshi, 85, 86, 88
yantra, 82
Yama, 64, 80, 80
Yami, 80
Yamantaka, 43, 69
Yamuna, 26
yana, 47
Yashodhara, 10, 35
Yellow Hat Order, 28, 71
Yeshe Tsogyal, 49, 52
yidam, x, 2, 69, 72, 73,
    76
yoga, 28, 47, 80, 82
Yogacara School, 28, 69
yogapatta, 59
yogasanas, 82
yogi, 49, 52, 54, 59
yogini, 54
yogis, tantric, deviant and
    confrontational behav-
    ior of, 59

zenith and nadir, 28
Zeus, 47

Other Publications from Binkey Kok

Singing Bowls
A Practical Handbook of Instruction and Use
Eva Rudy Jansen

The Book of Buddhas
Ritual Symbolism Used on Buddhist Statuary and Ritual Objects
Eva Rudy Jansen

The Book of Hindu Imagery
The Gods and their Symbols
Eva Rudy Jansen

Chinese Health Balls
Practical Exercises
Hans Höting

Didgeridoo
Ritual Origins and Playing Techniques
Dirk Schellberg

The Life of Buddha
Text by George Hulskramer
Illustrations by Bijay Raj Shakya and Raju Babu Shakya

The Joy of Drumming
Drums and Percussion Instruments from around the World
Töm Klöwer

Singing Bowl
Exercises for Personal Harmony
Anneke Huyser

CDs and Cassettes from Binkey Kok

Gong Meditation
Hans de Back

Chakra Meditation
Hans de Back

Hans de Back in Concert
Hans de Back

Singing Bowl Meditation
Hans de Back

Didgeridoo
Barramundi

The Purity of Sound
An acoustic Recording of Singing Bowls for Meditation
Rainer Tillmann

The Sounds of Planets/1
Meditation with the Planet Sounds of Tibetan Singing Bowls
Rainer Tillmann

The Sounds of Planets/2
Meditation with the Planet Sounds of Tibetan Singing Bowls
Rainer Tillmann

Sounds for Healing/1
Crystal and Tibetan Singing Bowls for Meditation and Healing
Rainer Tillmann

Sounds for Healing/2
Gongs and Tibetan Singing Bowls for Meditation and Healing
Rainer Tillmann